100 more of the world's best houses

of the world's best

100 more of the world's best houses

images
Publishing

Edited by Robyn Beaver

First reprinted in 2005
The Images Publishing Group Reference Number: 650

Published in Australia in 2005 by
The Images Publishing Group Pty Ltd
ABN 89 059 734 431
6 Bastow Place, Mulgrave, Victoria 3170, Australia
Tel: +61 3 9561 5544 Fax: +61 3 9561 4860
books@images.com.au
www.imagespublishing.com

Copyright © The Images Publishing Group Pty Ltd 2005
The Images Publishing Group Reference Number: 631

National Library of Australia
Cataloguing-in-Publication entry:

100 more of the world's best houses.

Includes index.
ISBN 1 920744 98 3.

1. Architecture, domestic – Pictorial works. 2. Interior decoration – Pictorial works.

728

Edited by Robyn Beaver

Designed by The Graphic Image Studio Pty Ltd, Mulgrave, Australia
www.tgis.com.au

Film by Mission Productions Limited
Printed by Everbest Printing Co. Ltd, in Hong Kong/China

Contents

222 Residence

Oklahoma, USA

ELLIOTT + ASSOCIATES ARCHITECTS

The owner was able to convince the developer to allow the construction of a "modern" house in a proposed "traditional" neighborhood. The conditions were that the modern house had to be invisible from the street and that the design would have to be approved by the local architectural review committee.

The architectural aim was to create a house that emerges from the earth, blending the site, soil, place, and form into an expression inspired by the unique conditions of this place and time.

The client's program wishes for the 3500-square-foot (325-square-meter) residence were detailed and precise. Included were requests for a "safe room" and sauna, an office for two people, a kitchen to accommodate a professional chef, exercise room, an outdoor living room, a lap pool, and a saltwater aquarium. Access into the house for the two family dogs was also mandatory.

Approach to the house begins with a curving, naturally landscaped entry road with a security "art" gate for monitored access to the house. A freestanding concrete wall with moveable, colored acrylic rods provides an ever-changing interactive arrival point at the front door. This, along with a 20 x 9-foot (6 x 3-meter) yellow steel frame, extends and captures visual fragments beyond the glass, blurring the distinction between indoors and outdoors.

The linear plan separates, and puts in sequence, public and private spaces with narrow glass connector spaces stitching them together. The spaces are created to provide unique personal moments in time, such as the view of a unique landscape feature from the bathtub or watching the wildlife from an exposed glass shower.

The interior finishes include a stained concrete slab the color of the soil, as if the site moves through the structure. Spatial warmth is created with surface and color. Above the kitchen counter is a glowing opening acting as art, and a man-made reminder of the seasons. Glass acts as an invisible separation to the natural world beyond, regardless of whether it is the shower, toilet, tub or kitchen. The glass garden on the north provides an unexpected pocket-sized Zen garden fashioned from recycled glass.

1 Public entry approach with rusting steel walls, gravel path and concrete entry wall
2 North patio with a sculptural steel frame to enhance view of landscape
3 Northwest corner illustrating the topography, site orientation, and the "floating" roof
4 West elevation with thrusting steel wall
5 Southwest corner view into the master tub area and exercise room

1

2

3

4

5

10

6

7

8

6 Master tub with eye-level glass
7 Kitchen view showing mahogany cabinets and light panel
8 Main entry showing rusted steel bridge and vision to the
     landscape beyond
9 Master bedroom with sculptural television cabinet
10 Living room looking west toward master bedroom
11 Floor plan
Photography: Hedrich Blessing

9

10

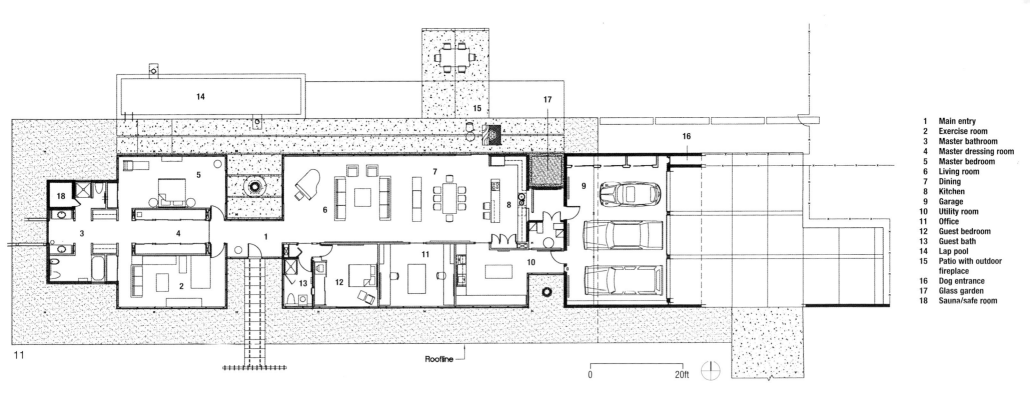

11

14

15

17

16

9

18

5

3

4

1

2

13

12

11

10

8

7

6

1	Main entry
2	Exercise room
3	Master bathroom
4	Master dressing room
5	Master bedroom
6	Living room
7	Dining
8	Kitchen
9	Garage
10	Utility room
11	Office
12	Guest bedroom
13	Guest bath
14	Lap pool
15	Patio with outdoor fireplace
16	Dog entrance
17	Glass garden
18	Sauna/safe room

Roofline

0   20ft

700 Palms Residence

Venice, California, USA

STEVEN EHRLICH ARCHITECTS

This residence was designed as a flexible compound for large family gatherings and overnight guests. Key requirements were to maximize volume, light and privacy on a narrow urban lot, and employ sustainability and sensitivity to scale and context. Built of raw, honest materials appropriate to the bohemian grittiness of Venice, the house dissolves the barriers between indoors and out, creating multi-use spaces that fully exploit the benign climate.

The site is a 43 x 132-foot (13 x 40-meter) lot on the corner of a street of traditional beach bungalows, lined with palms. At two stories plus a mezzanine level, the house, as well as its separate garage/guest house, is taller than most of its neighbors. The mass has been peeled back and mitigated on the upper levels by two large sheltering pine trees and a palm, one of which graces each of three distinct courtyards. Walls and landscaping screen the two street façades.

The wood-and-steel frame structure is outlined by a steel exoskeleton, from which automatic light scrims roll down to shield the front façade from the western sun. The 16-foot-high (5-meter) living/dining area opens up on three sides: to the lap pool on the west with sliding glass doors; to the north courtyard and guest house with pocketing glass doors; and to the garden to the south through pivoting metal doors. When opened entirely to the elements, the structure is an airy pavilion, with temperate ocean breezes making air-conditioning unnecessary. The concrete slab absorbs the sun's warmth in the winter and has a radiant heat source for cold nights, and photovoltaic panels at the roofline store and augment energy.

Shifts from confined to lofty spaces animate the design. Space is compressed at the low front entrance of the house, and then explodes into the main volume. Stairs lead up to a pair of mezzanine-level sleeping/lounging lofts with decks; a glass bridge spans the living room and leads to another flight of stairs up to the master bedroom and study. The top floor is flooded with light from a shed roof that opens a long clerestory to the western sky.

Rough and smooth surfaces contrast throughout the house. The western front façade, a clearly defined mass, is clad inside and out in Corten steel. Ample roof overhangs and fascias are of metal and parklex. The interior back wall of shot-blasted structural concrete masonry is a backdrop for artwork.

1

2

1 Corten steel panels
2 Pivot doors open to heated concrete platform
3 Glass slides into wall pockets
4 Concrete slab is radiant-heated

3

4

14

5

6

7

8

9

10

11

12

1	Living space	11	Bedroom
2	Pool	12	Bathroom
3	Entry	13	Deck
4	Powder room	14	Library
5	Dining room	15	Closet
6	Kitchen	16	Master bathroom
7	Laundry	17	Master bedroom
8	Storage	18	Kitchenette
9	Garage	19	Open to below
10	Bridge		

0   12ft

5   Shades protect from western sun

6   Indoor space fuses to courtyard and studio/guesthouse

7   Door slides fully connecting the bedroom to the terrace

8   Second level floor plan

9   Mezzanine level floor plan

10   Ground level floor plan

11   Glass wall slides away and external shades provide privacy

12   A glass bridge is suspended by stainless steel nautical cables

Photography: Erhard Pfeiffer (1,2,4,5,7,11,12);
Julius Schulman & Juergen Nogai (3,6)

Armadale House

Armadale, Victoria, Australia

JACKSON CLEMENTS BURROWS ARCHITECTS

This project involved alterations and additions to an existing Victorian house that had been renovated in the late 1980s. The client brief called for a new second-floor addition comprising five bedrooms and associated bathrooms. An extension of this requirement was to reconfigure the ground floor living, dining and kitchen areas. A critical factor in the reorganization of these spaces was to consider how the proposed alterations and additions could engage with a large external garden.

The original Victorian U-shaped plan configuration was rediscovered and reinforced by a first-floor addition that follows the outline of the perimeter walls below. As a gesture toward connecting the house to the garden and vice-versa, the two outer bedroom wings of the upper-floor addition cantilever beyond the ground floor to engage with the landscape.

To further reinforce this gesture at the ground-floor level, a large deck area projects into the garden. This provides a new outdoor living space defined by a stone wall and fireplace—an undercroft beneath the first-floor cantilevered bedroom wing.

The definition of the once-Victorian house is maintained as a rendered masonry construction type with punched openings framing views to the courtyard and garden beyond. The first-floor addition is a lightweight, timber-framed construction type with vertical cedar shiplap boards as cladding. The lightweight timber material and construction type provides a strong contrast to the masonry walls below. A black painted parallel flange channel separates the two materials as a shadowline and accentuates the cantilever of the first-floor bedroom wings on either side of the courtyard.

The first-floor window openings of the new works alternate between a lower and higher position, one scaled for adults and one for children, activating the corridor space.

1

1 Master bedroom wing and children's wing cantilever toward garden
2 Existing ground floor masonry forms embrace and protect the courtyard
3 The undercroft beneath the first floor provides a covered outdoor living space

2

3

4

4 Highlight windows provide natural light and define separation between old and new
5 Kitchen extends through living room to outdoor fireplace
6 Main dining room
7 First floor plan
8 Ground floor plan
9 Master bedroom ensuite

Photography: John Gollings, Gollings Photography Pty Ltd

5

6

1 Games/rumpus room
2 Bathroom
3 Walk-in robe
4 Master bedroom
5 Deck
6 Bedroom

7

1 Entry
2 Study
3 Cloak room
4 Formal lounge
5 Office
6 Formal dining
7 Courtyard
8 Deck
9 Living
10 Kitchen
11 Pantry
12 Powder room
13 Laundry
14 Bathroom
15 Guest bedroom
16 Garden/lawn
17 Existing studio

8

9

Atlanta Residence

Atlanta, Georgia, USA

OLSON SUNDBERG KUNDIG ALLEN ARCHITECTS

This new house in an historic Atlanta neighborhood uses modern materials to express the mystique of the old South. Traditional elements found in historic Southern mansions—front columns, a portico, Palladian spatial arrangement and an emphasis on the staircase—were reinterpreted to subtly connect the house to the region's strong architectural heritage. Space flows freely from inside to outside, and vistas amplify the sense of space on this relatively narrow urban lot.

1

2

3

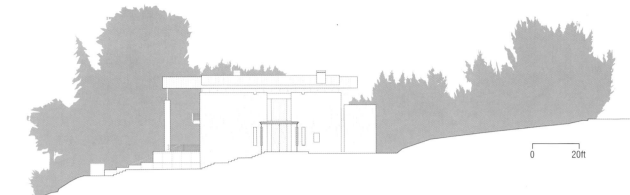

4

5

6

1 View toward living room
2 Façade facing wooded backyard
3 Central staircase inspired by those found in
   antebellum mansions
4 Street façade featuring reinterpreted portico
5 West elevation
6 Informal sitting room facing woodland garden
Photography: Scott Jenke (1,2,6); Bruce Van Inwegen (3,4)

B-Hive

Perth, Western Australia, Australia

HARTREE + ASSOCIATES ARCHITECTS

The B-Hive house reaches out and touches, indeed is almost immersed in, Perth's beautiful Swan River. The river becomes one with the sanctuary—a visual, physical and spiritual playground.

The architects' intention was to redefine the Australian veranda, to condition the relationship between inside and out, and to encourage the design to breathe freely. Internal spaces spill out physically and visually to adjacent outdoor spaces, with views to other components of the building helping to extend internal volumes.

Concealing glass panes within the stonework, the Arcadian family room converts to a riverside veranda, formed like a luxury boat deck. The success of this space, extending to the infinity-edge swimming pool and beyond, is achieved through a gentle transition at floor level, promoting a safe and continuous passage to the outdoors. Incorporating craftsmanship abandoned in the previous century, the stone portal stands proud, framing views of the ever-changing Swan River and capturing the daily theater of family life.

1

2

3

4

5

6

1 Seamless transition from indoors to outdoors
2 Riverfront
3 Arcadian family room transforms into a riverside veranda
4 Entry courtyard
5 Breezeway, tennis pavilion
6 The perfect setting for conversation, swimming and wasting time pleasurably

Photography: Robert Frith, Acorn Photo Agency

24

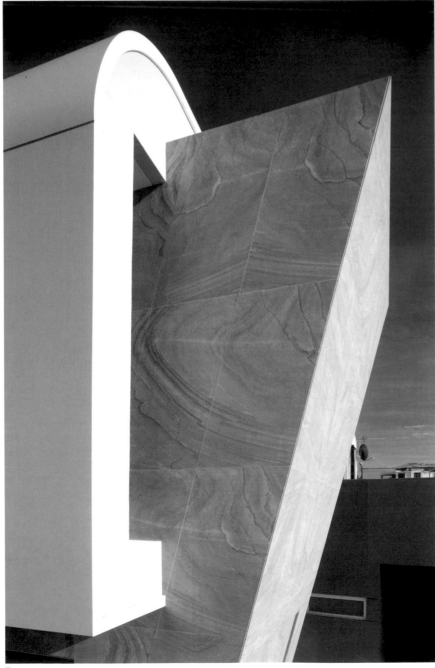

7

8

9

10

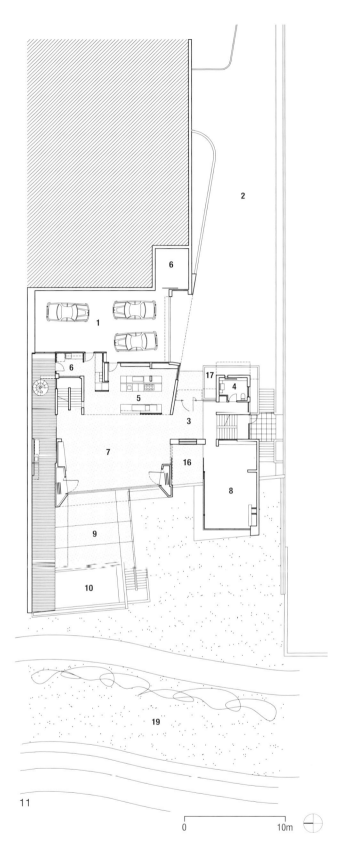

11

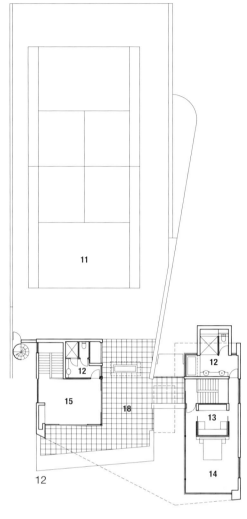

12

1	Garage/store
2	Driveway
3	Entry
4	Powder room
5	Kitchen
6	Laundry
7	Living/dining
8	Living/library
9	Pool deck
10	Pool
11	Tennis court
12	Bathroom
13	Walk-in robe
14	Bedroom
15	Sunroom
16	Deck
17	Reflection pond
18	Breezeway
19	River foreshore

0   10m

Baan Limpa

Koh Samui, Thailand

CL3 ARCHITECTS LTD

Located on a remote resort island in Thailand, Baan Limpa, ("Cliff Villa" in Thai) is, as its name implies, constructed on the side of a very steep hill. With spectacular ocean views, the owner had it custom-built as a holiday home and also for entertaining friends. Because of the requirement for privacy for visiting friends, and the constraints of the steep site, which required the structure to be broken down into a series of small stepped floorplates, the design evolved into a twin-villa design, one for the owner and the other for visiting guests.

The two villa wings are situated one on top of the other, guaranteeing unobstructed views and complete privacy. Each villa wing has its own pool and living spaces. The villas are built into the hillside and the layout was shifted during construction to safeguard existing boulders and trees, and to nestle the property into the steep terrain. Outdoor living is celebrated and every room has unobstructed sea views. Each villa wing consists of three private bedrooms, each with an ensuite, indoor living room, an open air "sala", and a black infinity-edge pool.

Entry to each villa wing is through a stone wall built of local black granite, and covered with a wooden trellis above. The entrance opens onto the sala, an open-air lounge with a teak wood roof, equipped with a bar and large daybed. From this level a flight of steps leads to the swimming pool and sun deck. The pool is clad in locally made black ceramic tiles and has an infinity edge on two sides. Sandstone slabs float on the pool and act as circulation linkage to the sun deck. The living and dining space is connected to the sun deck. Full-height glass doors with timber frames enclose the living space, and can be opened up fully. The swimming pool edge comes up to the side of the living space.

With a very simple color palette and choice of locally found material, the villa conveys a tropical and relaxed atmosphere. The bathroom fixtures and flooring are beautiful hand-tooled terrazzo. The walls are a combination of black slate and whitewash. Local art works and artifacts are incorporated to add a touch of Thai to the design.

1 Master bedroom with custom-designed platform bed
2 Open sala with bar in foreground
3 Black granite entrance wall with wooden trellis
4 Sun deck and infinity-edge swimming pool
5 Exterior view of villas
6 Main stair leading from entrance to pool area
Photography: Eddie Siu

1

2

4

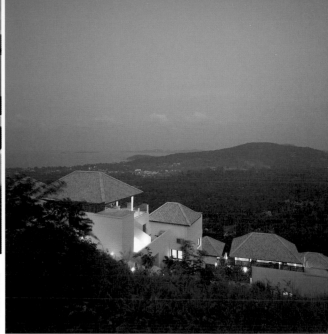

5

3

6

Bangkok House

Bangkok, Thailand

JACKSON CLEMENTS BURROWS ARCHITECTS IN ASSOCIATION WITH HASSELL LIMITED THAILAND

This 7532-square-foot (700-square-meter), two-story residence is located in central Bangkok, Thailand. The brief was to design a substantial family house that would offer withdrawal and sanctuary from the hectic nature of the surrounding city.

The site is located within a gated residential precinct with adjacent buildings presenting their backs to the site—an unimpressive collage of balconies, downpipes, air-conditioning condensers, water tanks and clothes lines. This condition provided an opportunity to explore a courtyard house typology, in this case, two linear forms shield the primary outdoor space.

Entry is through a double-height breezeway that connects the two forms. This space opens on axis to the swimming pool and courtyard garden beyond. Here a choice is made to proceed into either of two wings: to the left the informal living area surrounds a functional kitchen and scullery with a generous adjoining study; a master bedroom suite and guest bedroom suite are located above on the first floor. To the right is a formal lounge and entertaining area serviced by a bar. The first floor accommodates the children's bedrooms, study, and rumpus areas. Service spaces, housing housekeeper's quarters, a double garage, laundry and steam room for the pool, discreetly adjoin both wings.

This house attempts to embrace the tropical climate through provision of various private outdoor retreat spaces. The key zone uniting the house is the courtyard garden, which benefits from shade and offers a comfortable outdoor seating space. This space links the two ground-floor living areas and informal meals often occur in this location. The seating area is protected by a floating roof that provides filtered shade and allows use during frequent rain. Upstairs, the primary bedrooms also address protected decks with elevated garden views—private retreat spaces which can be occupied individually. The house can be cross-ventilated in two directions, minimizing the need for air-conditioning when possible. This cooling process is assisted by openable doors and windows located adjacent to the pool. The house often remains completely open to the courtyard, blurring the distinction between inside and out.

This house, through its interpretation of the courtyard typology, offers a unique variation on Asian central city life. Separation is provided by independent retreat spaces, but unity is achieved in the central courtyard space which draws the occupants to its subconscious microclimate—a unique sense of place which seems to remove any awareness of the city beyond.

1 Entry through breezeway
2 Kitchen and dining area
3 Lounge and entertaining areas
4 Elevation to streetscape
5 Study

1

2

3

4

5

6

8

7

9

6   Outdoor living area
7   Bar
8   Games room
9   Master bedroom ensuite
10 First floor plan
11 Ground floor plan
Photography: John Gollings, Gollings Photography Pty Ltd

1	Entry	14	Dining
2	Garage	15	Study
3	Lounge	16	Pool
4	Billiards	17	Outdoor living
5	Bar	18	Guest bedroom suite
6	WC	19	Ensuite
7	Laundry	20	Robes
8	Steam room	21	Master bedroom
9	Housekeeper	22	Bedroom suite
10	WC	23	Study
11	Living	24	Bedroom
12	Kitchen	25	Rumpus/bedroom
13	Scullery	26	Decks

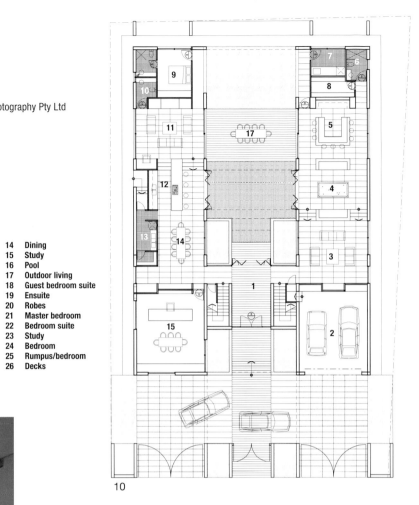

10

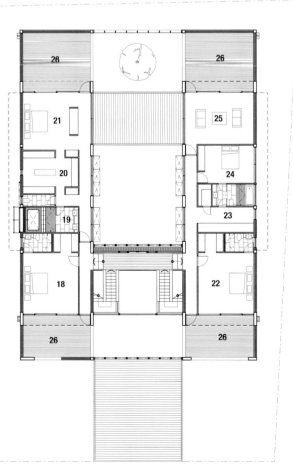

11

Beach Retreat

Paroa Bay, Bay of Islands, New Zealand

PETE BOSSLEY ARCHITECTS

In the far north of New Zealand, the Bay of Islands is a paradise of secluded bays and inlets. Located on a small farm at the western end of a bay, this house is for clients who desired a place with substance combined with a high degree of openness to the view and the landscape. With this house, the architects have developed their theme of "encampment," where the total house is fragmented into a series of smaller elements, defining a space between. A main living wing and three "sleepouts," each with its own living area, form the residence. The space between the four buildings becomes the focus for summer living, and a large covered terrace adjacent to the main living rooms is the heart of family life, with a 16-seat dining table, fireplace, barbeque and fish-cleaning facilities.

The scale of the 7962-square-foot (740-square-meter) house is reduced by the use of smaller elements, with the primary building resting in the valley and fronting the sea, and the sleepouts forming a bracelet of buildings nestled in to the steep hillside. In-situ concrete is used to anchor the buildings to the site, especially the sleepouts, which are dug in to the hillside. Long grasses from the surrounding paddocks are concentrated on the roofs of two of the sleepouts, while on the third, the turf extends onto the roof, forming a small peninsula to further define the outdoor spaces.

Further inland, a large shed, also built of concrete, and partially recessed into the hillside, reinforces the bay form of the overall ensemble. Beyond is the tennis court and further up the valley the caretaker's house, and farm buildings. Large areas of native bush are being restored, and pest control has ensured that populations of rare kiwi have begun to regenerate.

The central focus of the composition is the parabolic roof floating above the main living area, a delicate form which reflects light by day and night. As it is viewed from different directions it ranges from tightly opposed curves to a long slender plane hovering gracefully across the space below. At night concealed uplights shine across the warped white plane and provide drama internally and from outside.

Large overhangs, timber pergolas and sliding shutters ensure the walls of glazing are not overexposed to solar gain, and covered terraces to the north and south of the house provide shelter from whichever prevailing winds blow, while still providing the all-important connection to the sea. Frequent incorporation of high-level opening windows ensures natural cooling from cross-flow ventilation.

1 The three wings
2 The site
3 Main house at night
4 Elevations
5 Wing two
6 Outdoor living area
7 Living area of the main house
8 Ensuite bathroom
Photography: Patrick Reynolds

1

2

3

6

4

7

5

8

Belvedere Residence

Belvedere, California, USA

CCS ARCHITECTURE

Located right along the Bay, this project is a total and complete renovation of a two-story residence—the primary home for a family of five—and includes the development of the entire site from fence to fence and from street to water.

The dramatic setting and orientation of the site drove the design for this project. Starting from the street, an axis leads to the house, pierces it as a two-story central hall, and continues to the bay as a dock, aligning with Mt Tamalpias across the water. This 'through-axis' organization creates strong spatial connections to the water on the north and to the landscape of the site on the south. This also results in an enlargement of the overall perception, which posits the dichotomy of land versus water. This same organization occurs in two parallel ways—where flanking the central hall are living and dining on one side, kitchen and family on the other—both with equal width openings at opposite ends which establish the connections to the landscape and the water.

The second floor consists of three bedrooms with panoramic views of Marin and the immediate landscape. The site's landscape is a combination of limestone paving, lawn, and contained planting. The existing mature olive trees were relocated throughout as elements of scale, balance, and Mediterranean reference. The interior is a restrained palette of crisp white walls playing off limestone floors, natural wood, and steel.

1

2

1 Outdoor patio
2 Kitchen
3 Hallway with deck and waterfront beyond

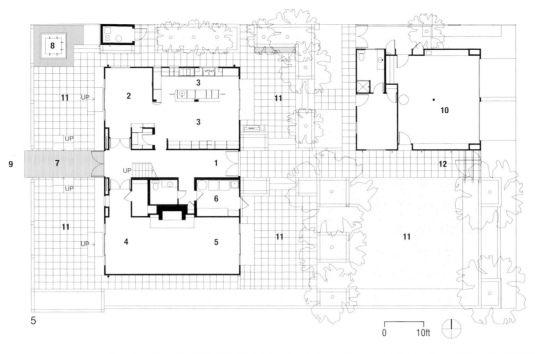

Opposite:
  Façade at dusk
5 Ground floor plan
6 Living room
Photography: Cesar Rubio

1 Entry
2 Family room
3 Kitchen/breakfast
4 Dining room
5 Living room
6 Utility room
7 Deck/dock
8 Jacuzzi
9 San Francisco Bay
10 Garage/guest
11 Site landscape
12 Entry/gate

0   10ft

5

6

Berkus Residence

Santa Barbara, California, USA

B3 ARCHITECTS

1 Front elevation presents a contemporary
   interpretation of Spanish Colonial form
2 View from living area to historic landmark,
   the Santa Barbara courthouse
3 Rear courtyard
4 Entry gallery
5 Oval library
Photography: Farshid Assassi (1,4); Peter Malinowski (2,3,5)

Constrained by a 29-foot-wide (9-meter) inner city site, and rigorous zoning and historical landmark board guidelines, this three-story custom dwelling begins the revival of single-family, detached downtown living in a historical district. The exterior of white stucco, iron, stone-clad colonnade, and tile roof is in keeping with Santa Barbara's Spanish Colonial architectural fabric, while modern and minimalist shapes reference the dignified, yet simple forms found in Viennese Secession architecture of the early 20th century.

Entry to the 3700-square-foot (344-square-meter) residence begins through a brightly colored indoor–outdoor entry court with mosaic floor patterning, leading to a 26-foot-long (8-meter) vaulted gallery and oval story-and-a-half library. The elevator and stair foyer act as the main circulation hub with access to the first-floor visiting artist's studio and living quarters, as well as to the second- and third-floor spaces. The main living and dining functions are situated within an open loft plan on the second floor, accommodating large gatherings and symposiums or intimate family living.

The master bedroom is fashioned as an enclosed retreat off the open plan. Live/work spaces and roof gardens cap the structure on the third floor. View planes are oriented to capture predominant architecture within the city, and third-floor overlooks capture an additional distant landscape of the city, mountain and ocean.

1

2

3 5 4

Bernal Heights Residence

San Francisco, California, USA

CCS ARCHITECTURE

This remodel of an existing three-story house transforms the interior with an airy, free-flowing space for living that opens to sweeping southern views of San Francisco.

The house was streamlined into three distinct and rejuvenated tiers for different aspects of the client's life. The ground floor work focused on entry improvements and a garage structural upgrade to accommodate the client's collection of vintage cars. The third floor was renovated as the most private part of the house, offering a master bedroom and two guest bedrooms to be grown into as the client looks forward to a future family. Between the two is the second floor—a new focal point of living, cooking, dining. This space—the center of most of the work—opens up the house's full floor area to daylight and southern views over San Francisco. Nearly all walls were removed and the floor was reorganized as a single contiguous space, half of which gathers at a monolithic, minimal kitchen-island. The client loves to cook and eat with friends; the new second floor responds with generous space for informal entertaining while cooking, as well as a stretch of dining area along the length of the house. Here, the southern exterior wall has been stripped open by a ribbon of windows and a glass door that will access a future deck over the backyard. By contrast, the north wall of the floor is lined with an understated but playful grid of shelves for books, artifacts from the client's travels, a stereo system, and liquor.

The second floor forms a center for the house, both a place to gather and to be sent back out to the city. It also contains many functions for living—both present and future—within a space that feels essentially open, airy and uncluttered.

1 Kitchen and island seating
2 Living room with dining area beyond
3 Open kitchen and dining plan for
   informal entertaining
4 Living room
5 Bedroom
Photography: Eric Laignel

1

2

3

4

5

Berry House

Atlanta, Georgia, USA

WILLIAM T. BAKER & ASSOCIATES

The Berry House is located in Druid Hills, a historic Atlanta neighborhood originally laid out by Frederick Law Olmstead, one of America's greatest landscape architects. The neighborhood's focal points are its Olmstead chain of parks bordered by wide tree-lined streets and the Druid Hill Golf Club. The Berry House is located on a quiet street that adjoins the golf course with park views at the front, and views of the golf course fairways at the rear.

The clients wanted their house to blend in with those surrounding it, especially the English-style homes from the 1920s. They had originally planned to purchase an original home but when they could not find one to suit their needs, decided that building a new "old" house was the best approach. The clients knew they had achieved that goal when a passerby asked how long it had taken to renovate this old house.

The two-story house features hand-carved limestone, a heavy variegated slate roof, and old-world brick. Superb interior detailing completes its authenticity.

1 Front elevation
2 Rear elevation

1

44

1	Foyer	15	Garage
2	Living room	16	Closet
3	Dining room	17	Front terrace
4	Powder room	18	Service entrance
5	Sun room	19	Butler's pantry
6	Kitchen	20	Covered porch
7	Breakfast	21	Bedroom
8	Family room	22	Bathroom
9	Laundry room	23	Media room
10	Gallery	24	Linen
11	Library	25	Upper hall
12	Master suite	26	Exercise room
13	Master bathroom	27	Open terrace
14	Elevator	28	Storage

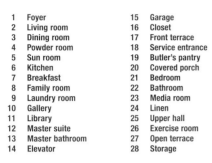

3

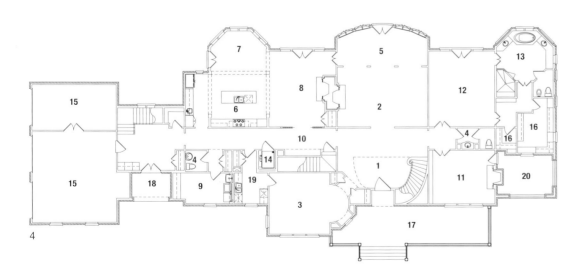

4

5

6

3   Second floor plan
4   First floor plan
5   Linenfold paneled library
6   Living room
7   Foyer
Photography: James Lockheart, Stone Mountain, Georgia

Black Residence

Cottesloe, Western Australia, Australia

CHINDARSI ARCHITECTS

Sited a few houses back from the beach at South Cottesloe, the starting point for this dwelling was a combination of a glazed pavilion in the garden as a "platform for living" and a thick wall for containment of the service and private functions.

The house looks inward to the internal courtyard and plunge pool on the ground floor, and inversely looks outward on the upper level. Vertical connection through the main staircase links the basement with the ground and first floors. The house was conceptually divided into a "service wall" running along the eastern length of the site which houses the more private spaces of bedrooms and wet areas, and a "garden pavilion" that houses the open-plan living and dining areas. The lower level playroom opens via an oversized sliding glass door into the courtyard and plunge pool area, with the polished concrete floors extending outside to blur the boundary between inside and out. The upper level living room and alfresco balcony platform are stepped up from the rest of this level to define the pavilion from the wall, and enable views across the roofline to the Indian Ocean beyond.

Options for openings for the entry of light were explored. Some openings were punched or carved with angled reveals out of the conceptual thick wall spaces. Other openings were created by "folding" other walls: the front "hanging" orange wall creates a butterfly as it folds open to take in views up and down the street, while still maintaining privacy for the occupants at street level.

Brightly painted Australian vernacular fibro beach-shacks as well as the strong colors used by the Mexican architect Ricardo Legorreta were the inspiration for the colored walls to the dwelling, and were an attempt to subvert the suburban nature of the surrounding dwellings.

Passive solar design principles were considered, although the block has a long north–south axis, which isn't ideal for minimizing heat gain. The desire to maximize the view to the west contradicted the need to minimize openings on the east- and west-facing walls. Generous eave overhangs were incorporated where possible over windows. Over the largest west-facing window to the first floor living area, two remote-controlled external sunscreens were installed, which significantly cut heat and glare while still allowing views through the semi-transparent fabric.

1 View of front pedestrian entry up toward the alfresco balcony
2 From street level, the orange butterfly wall hangs over a forest of Chinese tallow trees
3 The raised level of the open garden pavilion houses the main living and alfresco balcony area to the north

4

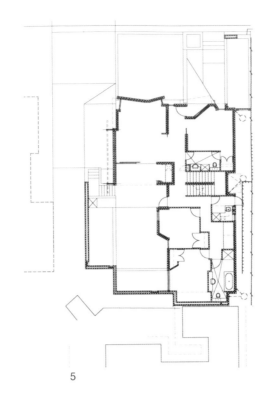

5

6

0   10m

7

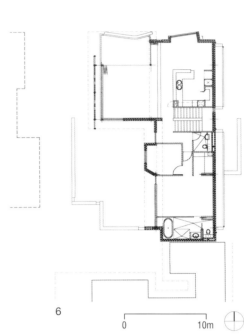

8

4   The master bedroom–ensuite relationship offers
    unrestricted views to Rottnest Island, just off the coast
5   Ground floor plan
6   First floor plan
7   A glow of turquoise from the plunge pool fills the ground
    floor courtyard
8   Light from the setting sun fills the open-plan upper-level
    living/dining/kitchen area
Photography: Robert Frith – Acorn Photo Agency

Botanic Gardens House

Singapore

GUZ ARCHITECTS

Perched on top of an expansive sloping site and overlooking the botanical gardens, the client's brief for the design of the house was clear: to allow spaces to flow between indoors and outdoors, and to fully exploit the feeling of openness and living in the tropics. The architectural concept of layering was employed to mold the shape of the 10,760-square-foot (1000-square-meter) house. In plan, this translates into three main spaces: the entrance foyer; the garden and pool; and the activity rooms. In section, it is a descending tier with the double-story wing of the entrance block looking out over the landscaped garden and pool, and then onto the single-story pavilion of the second block. All three spaces overlook the botanical gardens below. All the enclosed spaces are designed to integrate with the landscape outside. Covered veranda spaces and green roof terraces overlooking the pool and garden are conceived as entertainment and relaxation zones to maximize the pleasure of tropical living. By minimizing internal partitions, the architect achieves a seamless flow of breeze, light and shadow within the living spaces.

With each space having their own distinct functions, the tactile qualities of the living spaces are differentiated through the use of warm, natural materials, landscaping and detailing. The architect's sensitivity to the owner's needs and anticipated movement through the house inform the spatial layout and form, generating a number of secondary routes within the primary circulation. Traveling through the house, one's sensitivity is heightened by the changes in mood and the quality of light and one's journey becomes a poetic experience.

1 Veranda seat overlooking the drop off
2 View across pool to living area
3 Attic and roof garden
4 View across pool to entrance court
Photography: Luca Tettonni/guz architects

1

2

3

Brosmith Residence

Beverly Hills, California, USA

ZOLTAN E. PALI, FAIA; STUDIO PALI FEKETE ARCHITECTS (SPF:a)

The Brosmith Residence sensitively sites a single-family residence on a ridgeline of Mulholland Scenic Parkway, overlooking the San Fernando Valley of southern California. In accordance with the client's objectives, the structure captures exterior space as living space, and harnesses the panoramic views of the valley below, accessible from the common areas and courtyards of the property. Separate living pods along a central spine of the 5000-square-foot (465-square-meter) house allow different activities and interactions to occur simultaneously without mutual disruption. Each living pod is outfitted with its own version of an indoor–outdoor courtyard space, and each is connected independently to the central spine of the house. Pods are designed around the master suite, the children's quarters, offices, and caretaker's quarters. Entering into the common living areas, one is met with breathtaking vistas of the San Fernando Valley, climaxing on the main patio where a glass-like swimming pool disappears entrancingly over the crisp clean horizon of the site's northern edge.

The energy-conserving structure uses passive siting and natural shading to reduce its dependence on mechanical environmental conditioning systems. Courtyards are located to take advantage of prevailing breezes. Innovative uses of standard materials create much of the custom feel of this residence, where concept and design elevates the feel of every room. A sliding louvered screen in the master suite uses an off-the-shelf, affordable aluminum frame (echoed elsewhere in the house) fitted with aluminum louvers substituted for glass, creating a unique application that seamlessly integrates with the clean lines of the house.

1

2

3

1 Rear entry from pool patio
2 View of master bedroom window from pool
3 North-facing view from outside living room

54

5

6

1 Master bedroom
2 Master bathroom
3 Private patio
4 Dressing room
5 Living area
6 Dining area
7 Kitchen and breakfast area
8 Family room
9 Garage
10 Children's bedroom
11 Children's bathroom
12 Guest bedroom
13 Nursery
14 Patio
15 Laundry room
16 Powder room

0   10ft

7

Casa Hachem

São Paulo, Brazil

RAUL DI PACE

The "Jardim America" neighborhood of São Paulo, where this house is located, was designed in 1913. It was then, and is today, a model of urban intervention, offering a high standard of living to the owners of the lots, with their standard "house plus garden" configuration. In earlier times, the houses had low walls and formed a harmonious whole with their eclectic architecture and front gardens.

In 1913 this was a peripheral zone of São Paulo; today it is located in the area known as "the espandid center," surrounded by dense traffic. Consequently, the façade characteristics and the main access to the houses have changed, to provide improved safety and privacy for the resident families. The first house built on this lot was smaller, and surrounded by a beautiful garden, which has survived till now despite all the changes made to the house over the years.

In 2003 the architect was engaged to design a new project on the site. The existing house was comfortable but divided into small rooms with very few spaces opening to the outside and the garden was not used to its full capacity.

The architect's idea was to return to the original reference, of the house surrounded by a garden, bringing light to the inside, and creating a transparent environment with an expansive view of the garden. To achieve these goals, the masonry walls were transformed into glass walls with a steel structure, creating the transparency required for the new context. The visual boundaries of the house were thus transferred to the outer edge of the site, amplifying the sensation of space and aiming to recover part of the original concept of the English house and garden.

1 Bar and living area at night
2 House and swimming pool viewed from the garden
Opposite:
　House and swimming pool viewed from the gym area at night

1

2

58

4

5

6

7

8

Castle Groenhof

Belgium

SAMYN AND PARTNERS, ARCHITECTS AND ENGINEERS

The castle was built around 1830 in an asymmetrical French style. In accordance with the principles of building conservation, all the renovations were carried out so that they are potentially reversible, thereby maintaining the integrity of the original building.

The floor area of the three-level residence is 10,330 square feet (960 square meters). Internally, the ground floor consists of a south corridor, organized into a long and simple gallery that extends with a reflecting water surface across the park. The stair in the gallery extension leads to a north–south cross gallery both on the first and second floors, where a spiral stair leads to the terrace roof.

The roof features a wooden terrace and a parapet of steel rods, as well as a central glazed stairwell lantern, a canopy of glazed solar collectors for hot water, and stainless steel chimneys for natural ventilation of the bedrooms.

The south façade is balanced by the addition of a sophisticated glass and steel construction, that sits 9 feet (2.7 meters) away, parallel to the façade. The steel frame incorporates a glazed "orangerie" at ground-floor level, a permeable wooden terrace that spans to the existing façade, stainless steel solar screens at the first floor, and photovoltaic cells on clear glass sheets on the second floor.

1 Spiral stair landing on roof terrace
2 South façade with stainless steel solar shutters open
Opposite:
    East façade

1

2

4 Second floor plan
5 First floor plan
6 Ground floor plan
7 Main gallery at ground floor, looking west
8 Spiral staircase from second floor to roof terrace
9 Main south façade
Photography: Jan Verlinde (1,2,7,8); Ch. Bastin & J. Evrard (Opposite,9)

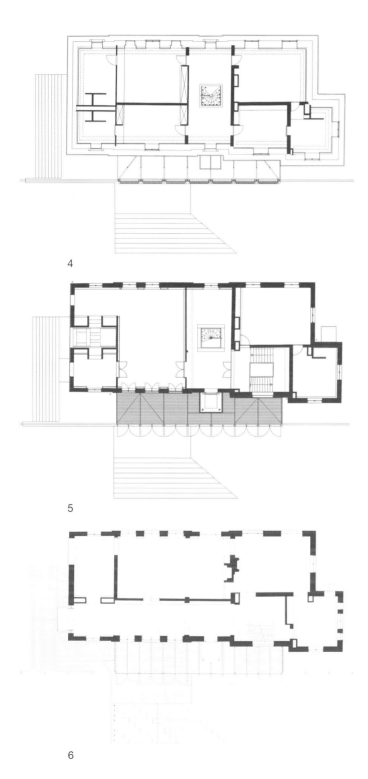

4

5

6

7

8

Cell Brick House

Tokyo, Japan

YASUHIRO YAMASHITA, ATELIER TEKUTO

The Cell Brick House sits on a corner lot in a tranquil Tokyo residential area. At first glance it appears to be a structure of concrete blocks, but closer inspection reveals the blocks to be steel boxes. Further examination reveals that this ingenious collection of steel boxes is in fact an amazing house. The architects call the construction "void masonry." The boxes serve not only as structure, but because they are left open on the inside, they can also be used as storage units in the house's interior. They also work to create brise-soleils, protecting the building from the heat of the environment.

The steel boxes measure approximately 35 x 18 x 12 inches (900 x 450 x 300 millimeters); the exterior surface is 3/8-inch (9 millimeters) thick and remaining walls are 1/4 inch (6 millimeters) thick. The boxes come in units of five or six, and are fused on site with high-tension steel bolts. The box units are assembled so that there are many openings, allowing dappled light to enter the interior. A special ceramic-infused material, developed by NASA, is used to coat the exterior steel plates, improving heat resistance.

The 915-square-foot (85-square-meter), three-level home was built for a designer and her son and daughter, both in their twenties. She suggested several novel ideas for the project, which the architect was able to realize, making the house even more remarkable. For example, the bathroom is situated so that it looks like it floats, and the washing machine sits on the way up a spiral staircase that links the three levels of the house.

1

1 A stumpy little tower on its tiny corner site
2 The house made of identical steel boxes coated with fused ceramic material
3 The washing machine is in the middle of the spiral stairway

2

3

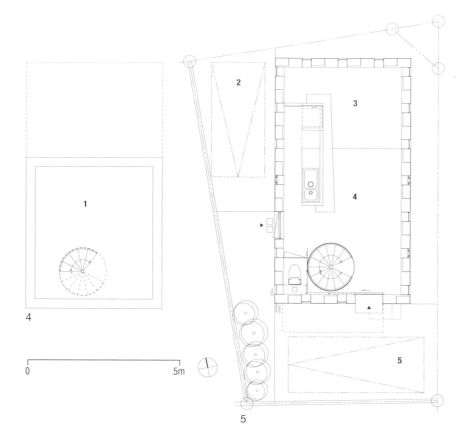

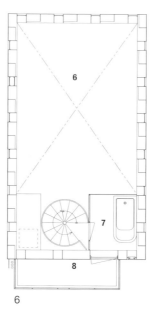

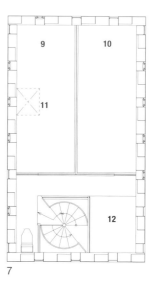

0   5m

4

5

6

7

8

1	Room 1	7	Bathroom
2	Car parking	8	Terrace
3	Bedroom	9	Room 2
4	Dining/living room	10	Room 3
5	Car parking	11	Skylight
6	Void	12	Loft

4–7   Floor plans
8   View from entrance
9   The builders chose to replace masonry with a system that utilizes stacked metal units
10   Looking down from the second floor
11   The 18 x 35 x 12-inch steel boxes (450 x 900 x 300 mm) provide ample storage
12   Stacked boxes form a checkerboard pattern
Photography: Makoto Yoshida

8

9

10

11

12

The Chameleon House

Michigan, USA

ANDERSON ANDERSON ARCHITECTURE

This prototype has been built on a small peninsula that juts into Lake Michigan. The house is part of a series of projects by the architects that explore the opportunities for using SIPs (Structural Insulated Panels) in cost-effective ways to build site-adapted structures from standardized components.

The system is designed to inexpensively accommodate a variety of complex site conditions with minimal disturbance to the natural topography, water flow, and vegetation. Although few restrictive or unusual zoning constraints exist at this location, the challenging topography and geotechnical conditions play a strong role in defining the overall design strategy. The small ground-floor building footprint/foundation reduces the cost and allows the foundation to step up the site with the slope of the hill.

The clients are a young couple with children who live several hours away from the site and will be using the house as a weekend retreat and vacation home. They wanted airy, open spaces where they could live and play together, and small bedrooms. The result is a small house of 1650 square feet (152 square meters), with nine different living levels.

To keep costs and on-site labor to a minimum, SIPs panels compose the exterior walls and roof structure, which also brings a high level of insulation. Although the panels are used as structural elements throughout, the addition of a two-story prefabricated steel moment frame on the lake view side allows for the double-height window wall and the open loft-like spaces within the main living area.

The house is carefully integrated into the rolling topography of its cherry orchard site. The site is minimally disturbed, other than the mounding of two earthen enclosures adjacent to the tower, created from the excavated earth of the foundation and offering a ground to contrast the tower experience above the treescape.

To help mask the scale, the building is wrapped in a skirting wall of recycled translucent polyethelene slats, standing 2 feet (0.6 meters) out from the galvanized sheet metal cladding of the wall surface on aluminum frames that serve also as window washing platforms and emergency exit ladders. The translucent polyethylene material set out over the dully reflective wall cladding is chosen for its ability to gather the light and color of its landscape. The double skin creates a microclimate and thermal differential around the structure, creating a rippling mirage updraft that in the summer emits clouds of steaming condensation or in the winter drips melting icicles.

1 Detail of exterior steel stair and polyethelene screen
2 View from south
3 View of house from the west
4 Northwest elevation
5 Southwest elevation
Photography: James Yochum

1

2

3

4

5

Chan Residence

West Vancouver, British Columbia, Canada

JAMES KM CHENG ARCHITECTS INC.

Recent empty-nesters, the clients desired a smaller home with all of the major living areas (including the master suite) on one level. For future resale value, additional bedrooms, guest rooms and a recreation area were to be provided on a separate level. Other requirements were that views be maximized and the interior be open and bright without the loss of privacy to the street. Ease of maintenance and security was a high priority. A special request was made for a secured and acoustically isolated room for listening to music.

The 5536-square-foot (514-square-meter) residence is sited so that every room is oriented toward the view of Vancouver. The exceptions are the guest room and recreation room in the lower level, which are oriented toward the bamboo court. With the southern orientation, large overhangs have been provided to reduce glare and to moderate summer heat gain. The living/dining room and the upstairs study and bedroom window walls have been slanted forward to reduce internal reflection and glare.

Interior layout is designed to maximize the indoor/outdoor relationship yet zoned to provide privacy when entertaining guests. Near views of the courtyard provide interest on gray days in addition to supplying a softer and diffused light source. All major rooms receive light from at least two directions. A special room of concrete with sloping acoustical ceilings at the northwest end off the entry satisfies the request for music listening.

This house is not air-conditioned. A sunken north-facing courtyard provides cooling in the summer while bringing a balanced light in from the north. The second-floor gallery provides additional summer air circulation through the greenhouse effect. The exterior walls are designed as rain-screens with airspace and insulation outboard. Materials were chosen for their low-maintenance characteristics: limestone, aluminum siding, and metal roofs. Wood windows were chosen for their warmth and thermal qualities. Interior finishes include limestone floors with radiant heat in all public areas and washrooms and carpet in bedrooms. Interior walls and ceilings in public areas are clad with limestone and wood to reduce the need for painting. Similarly, exterior plant materials such as bamboo, azaleas, rhododendrons and ground covers of ivy and wintergreen result in effortless gardening.

The layering of the courtyard and screens provide privacy from the road and the uphill neighbors, while retaining a sense of openness.

1 View of Vancouver from second floor hallway
2 South-facing rooms with generous overhang
3 Front entry and glass screen to sunken courtyard

1

2

4

4 View of family room/nook
5 View from second floor bedroom deck
6 View from entry hall
7 Upper level floor plan
8 Ground floor plan
9 Basement floor plan
Photography: Roger Brooks Photography

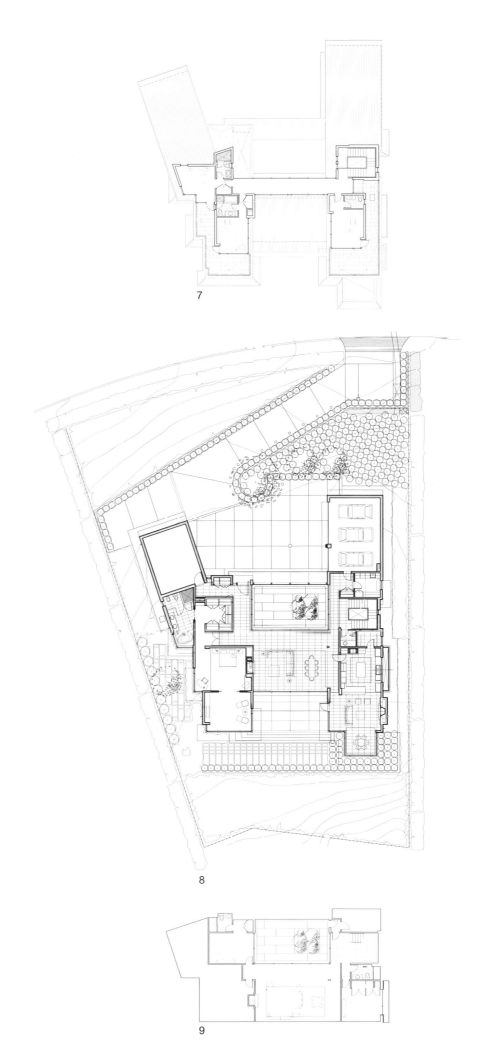

7

8

9

Chicago Town House

Chicago, Illinois, USA

ALEXANDER GORLIN ARCHITECTS

This town house for a bachelor in the Bucktown district of Chicago is a gleaming modern structure that floats above its more traditional neighbors. Set back behind a brick-walled garden, a steel and stone stair cuts through the volume of the house leading directly from the street to the main living level on the second floor and beyond to the third level and roof terraces above. On the main level, a double-height space contains the open loft of the kitchen, living, and dining areas. The vertically oriented living room is framed by large expanses of glass, which open onto the garden below and provide views of the street.

Above, the suspended glass box of the master bedroom and bathroom floats. The sensual space of the glass shower and freestanding tub is directly open to the master bedroom, blurring the boundaries between these traditionally separate areas. At both ends, glass walls afford views of the city. The clothes closet is completely open to view, where the client's perfectly coordinated suits hang for all the world to see, allowing him to "shop" daily for his suit of choice—recalling perhaps a scene from *American Gigolo*. Above is a terrace with views to downtown Chicago. A luminous screen of parachute cloth curtains—a theatrical gesture—defines the space of the dining room, with its own terrace above the garage. On the lower level are a guest bedroom and an exercise space. Materials are limited to a minimally cool palette of white painted steel, white statuary marble for all counters, gray-toned stone floors from China, and white plaster walls.

1 Theatrical setting of dining room with translucent
   parachute cloth curtains
2 & opposite:
   Floating cube of light: façade from Paulina Street

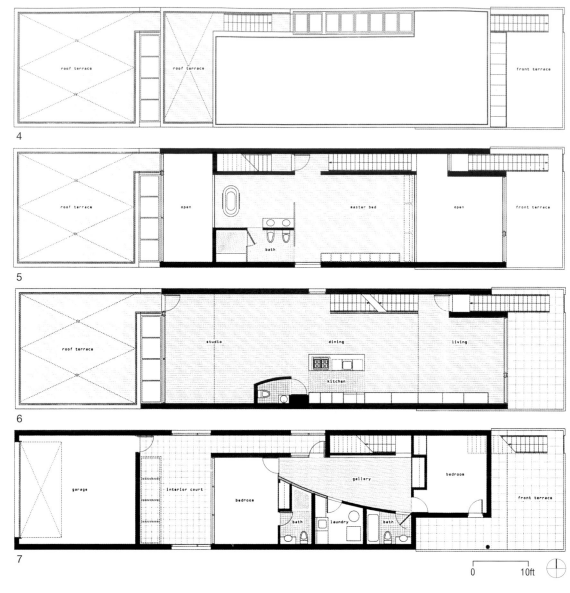

4

5

6

7

0 10ft

8

9

4   Roof plan
5   Second floor plan
6   First floor plan
7   Ground floor plan
8   View from dining room to kitchen and living room
9   Bathroom perpetuates home's theme: cubes of glass and light
10 Living room with view to bedroom and wardrobe/privacy screen
11 Skylight, stair to bedroom and rear terrace
Photography: Michael Moran

Conrad House

Sausalito, California, USA

SWATT ARCHITECTS

The Conrad House is built over the footprint of a 1950's residence by noted Bay Area modernist Roger Lee that over the years had suffered irreparable structural damage. The new design doubles the area of house to 2700 square feet (250 square meters) while maintaining the original emphasis on the expressive use of wood and the distribution of public and private spaces.

The site is a narrow, steep, up-sloping lot, heavily wooded on the hillside to the south, with unobstructed views to the north. The new residence works with its hillside site by providing direct access to outdoor areas and taking advantage of views of San Francisco Bay and Mt Tamalpais. The owners expressed a strong desire that wherever possible, the design must utilize natural materials left in their original state.

The new design retains the spirit of the original on the exterior and the interior through its expressive use of wood structure and finishes. Strip windows and cedar siding emphasize the horizontality of the design, extending the lines of the house into the site, and helping nestle the house into the hillside. Post-and-beam construction is used to reveal the structure of the house and articulate the grid upon which it is based. Tongue-and-groove cedar soffits visually connect interior spaces to decks and terraces beyond.

Interior details are simple and minimal, designed to strengthen the expression of post-and-beam construction. Dark gray limestone floors, precast concrete panels, brushed stainless steel counter tops and fireplace, and stainless steel cable rails contrast with and complement the warmer tones of the predominantly wood structure.

All major rooms are situated on the north side of the house to take advantage of the panoramic views. An expansive double-height stair hall on the south side of the house connects all major rooms and acts as a counterpoint to the horizontality of the rest of the design. This hall has a floor-to-ceiling window facing the hillside beyond that allows sunlight, filtered through a canopy of mature live oaks, to penetrate deep into the interior.

1

2

3

1 Kitchen
2 Entry at night
3 Overall view from northwest

4

5

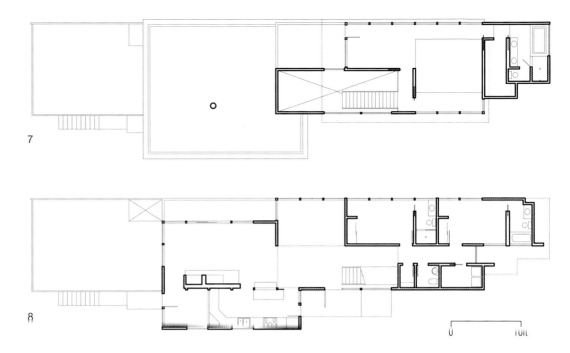

7

8

4   North elevation at night
5   Master bedroom and sitting area
6   Dining area and stair
7   Upper level floor plan
8   Lower level floor plan
9   View from master bedroom
Photography: Cesar Rubio

9

Copper House

Massachusetts, USA

CHARLES ROSE ARCHITECTS INC

The challenge of this renovation was to add a wing to an existing 1940's kit home. The original house was sited poorly on the south side of a 1-acre (0.4-hectare) hillside lot. An attached garage to the north obscured the spacious yard from the interior of the house. The garage was demolished and the addition was sited in its place. This siting preserved an east-facing terrace and created a west-facing entry court.

The design integrates and distinguishes between the old and new architectures. Formally, aesthetic dissonance is reduced by wrapping the original house in a monolithic, neutral cedar scrim; experientially, the historically inspired interior characteristics and small scale of the original structure are preserved.

The two-story addition is oriented east–west. The addition is opened to the site on the north, east, and west sides, and contains the main living spaces of the house, as well as the master bedroom and two offices on the second floor. A roof terrace with a hearth has panoramic views of the site and of Boston. A glass and steel stair connects the first and second floors, and an exterior stair leads to the roof deck from a deck off the master bedroom. A three-story skylit space mediates between the larger scale of the new and the smaller scale of the old, and serves as entry and circulation to the house.

Exterior construction materials include sheet copper, mahogany and Alaskan cedar windows, exposed aggregate concrete, painted steel, western red cedar siding, and bluestone. Interior materials include hardwood and bamboo floors, beech veneer paneling and casework, painted steel, and bluestone.

1 Detail view of north façade at living room
2 Entry court
3 View from northeast

1

2

4

6

4   View from upper level atrium looking east
5   Living room looking northeast
6   Living room looking west
7   Lower level floor plan
8   Upper level floor plan
9   View from kitchen toward dining area
Photography: John Edward Linden

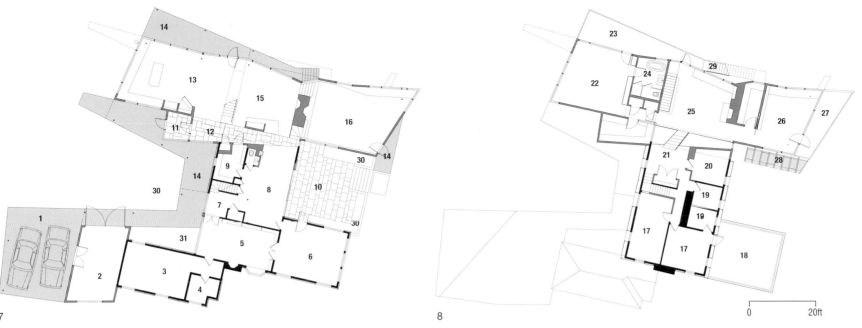

7

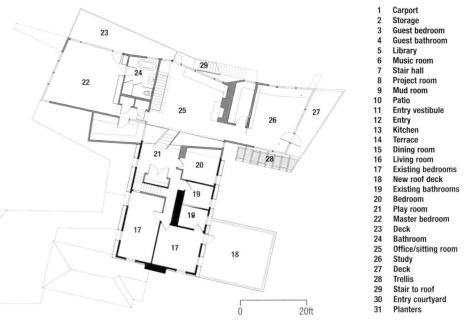

8

1	Carport
2	Storage
3	Guest bedroom
4	Guest bathroom
5	Library
6	Music room
7	Stair hall
8	Project room
9	Mud room
10	Patio
11	Entry vestibule
12	Entry
13	Kitchen
14	Terrace
15	Dining room
16	Living room
17	Existing bedrooms
18	New roof deck
19	Existing bathrooms
20	Bedroom
21	Play room
22	Master bedroom
23	Deck
24	Bathroom
25	Office/sitting room
26	Study
27	Deck
28	Trellis
29	Stair to roof
30	Entry courtyard
31	Planters

0   20ft

9

The Cray Shed

Pauanui, New Zealand

KOIA ARCHITECTS

What are the components of a perfect holiday home? Ample room for friends and family to congregate, and large, sheltered outdoor living spaces are at the top of most lists. So it was with The Cray Shed, a 4305-square-foot (400-square-meter) holiday home at Pauanui, on New Zealand's beautiful Coromandel Peninsula. A south-facing building site close to its neighbors, and the requirement that the house be large enough for two families to enjoy, posed some interesting challenges.

The solution was inspired by the simple shape of a boatshed, reflecting its waterfront location. It presents a secure face to the street, with the living spaces opening toward the canal. Full-height sliding doors offer views through the house and out over the water, admitting lots of light into the home despite its difficult orientation. Another key feature is the double-sided open fireplace in the glass wall overlooking the water. A big enclosed courtyard, again with an open fireplace, is tailor-made for entertaining al fresco. Wrapped around on three sides by the house, and with a high wall closing off the fourth side, it offers peace, privacy and protection from the prevailing southerly wind.

1

2

1 Landscaping is planned as a number of planted and hard surfaced terraces, allowing for generous entertainment areas and the occasional high tide
2 Broad stairs connect the home to the pontoon, to create a wharf-like aesthetic and generous access to the water
Opposite:
   The double-sided fire is enjoyable whether sitting inside or out

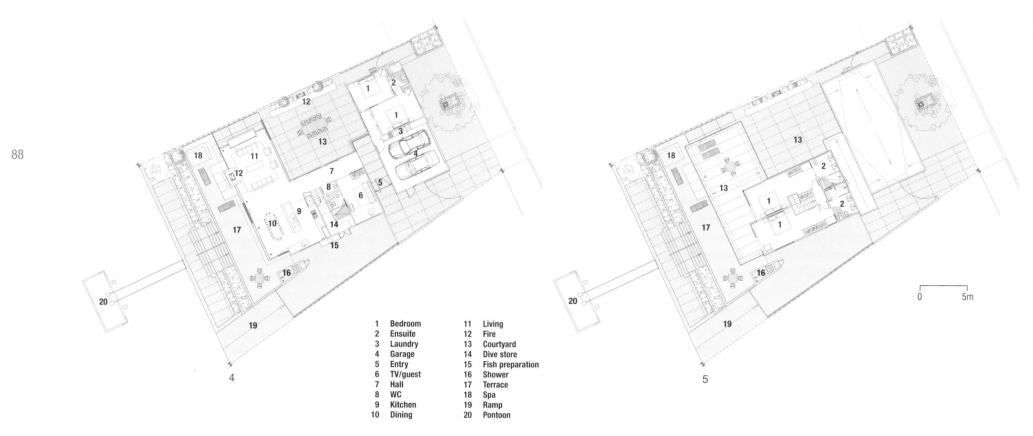

4

1	Bedroom	11	Living
2	Ensuite	12	Fire
3	Laundry	13	Courtyard
4	Garage	14	Dive store
5	Entry	15	Fish preparation
6	TV/guest	16	Shower
7	Hall	17	Terrace
8	WC	18	Spa
9	Kitchen	19	Ramp
10	Dining	20	Pontoon

5

0   5m

6

7

8

9

10

11

4 Ground floor plan

5 First floor plan

6 Living room is transparent to allow maximum views of the canal

7 Retractable doors to both sides create a tent-like living area

8 Indoor entertainment

9 View from canal

10 Cosy living

11 Sunny, sheltered courtyard provides a spot for year-round entertainment

Photography: Kallan MacLeod; photographs provided courtesy of Trends Publishing International

Crescent Road House

Toronto, Ontario, Canada

SUPERKÜL INC. ARCHITECT

With children grown up and with families of their own, the clients wanted to build a new home for themselves, tailored to the smaller scale of a two-person family.

Knowing they wanted to stay in the South Rosedale neighborhood they had been in for more than 30 years, but not able to find a suitable site on which to build, they severed their existing property. The resulting lot, measuring 44 x 138 feet (13.5 x 42.2 meters), contains an existing coach house at the rear and several mature trees.

The architect's intent was to design a modern townhouse that would comply with applicable setback and building height regulations and be a respectful intervention in the surrounding traditional fabric. To achieve this, materials and proportional relationships for the new house took their cues from neighboring houses. Red brick, dark wood siding, and bronze anodized window frames were used, the subdivision of the front façade and building massing respond to the adjacent houses, and a horizontal canopy defines the entrance forecourt addressing the gentle curve of the street.

The 2725-square-foot (250-square-meter) house has three principal volumes: two, two-story brick and wood boxes that contain and form a taller two-and-a-half story atrium in the center. The center atrium is the vertical and horizontal fulcrum of the design. It is the principal ordering element of the three main living spaces of the lower floor: kitchen/dining, atrium, and living room, and separates the different sleeping and study quarters of the upper floor. A glazed lantern tops the center atrium, bringing light deep into the middle of the house and providing for passive cooling and ventilation by convection with the use of motorized operable vents. An open stone staircase wraps around a lift that rises up the atrium leading to a mezzanine level overlooking the lower floor.

The existing coach house at the rear is restored and converted into a garage and hobby workshop space. An exterior court extends the interior space of the house to the outdoors. The wonderful 48-year-old magnolia tree at the front of the property, a well-recognized and highly appreciated tree in the community, especially when in bloom, remains.

1 Front elevation
2 Southwest front corner
3 West elevation

1

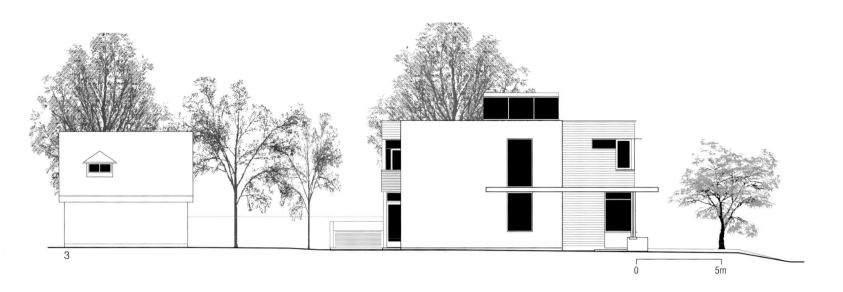

3

0   5m

2

Photography: Tom Arban

92

4

5

6

1	Front entry	9	Open to below
2	Living	10	Study/work desk
3	Atrium	11	Bedroom
4	Dining	12	Dressing
5	Kitchen	13	Balcony
6	Pantry/storage	14	Built-in barbeque
7	Lift	15	Courtyard
8	Mud room		

7

0   5m

8

9

Crystal Brick House

Tokyo, Japan

YASUHIRO YAMASHITA, ATELIER TEKUTO

A wooden house built some forty years ago had stood on this site. Since it had become dilapidated, it was demolished, but the steel-framed house behind it was left standing. The Crystal Brick house was built to connect to this remaining building.

Flat steel bars were assembled like a birdcage, and a combination of different kinds of glass blocks were stacked to form transparent, earthquake-resistant walls. There are no supporting pillars in the open-plan floor space.

The occupiers of this three-level, 1205-square-foot (112-square-meter) house are members of an extended family, including grandparents, parents, and two children. They had specified that the house was to be full of light. The architect's solution to this was to place transparent glass blocks over a base of translucent glass blocks, allowing people to see both inside and out while flooding the house with light. Opaque blocks were strategically used to provide privacy where required.

1

2

3

4

1	Entrance	8	Atelier	15	Room 1
2	Hall	9	Void	16	Room 2
3	Kitchen	10	Closet	17	Bedroom
4	Closet	11	Bathroom	18	Utility room
5	Bedroom	12	Walk-in closet	19	Kitchen
6	Bathroom	13	Hall	20	Dining/living room
7	Study	14	Entrance	21	Balcony

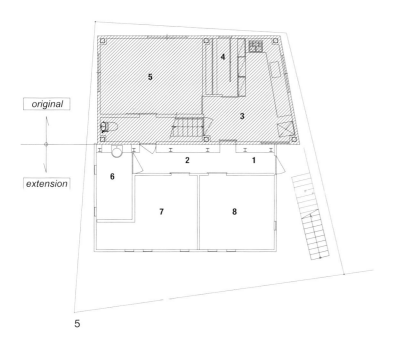

original

extension

5

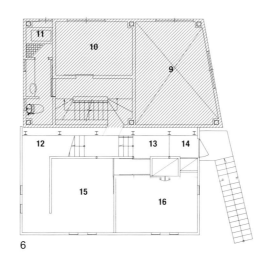

6

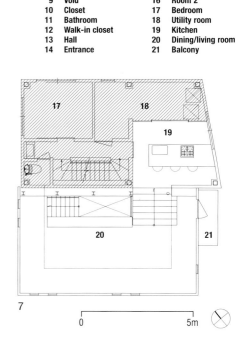

7

0   5m

8

9

1   Night view from south
2   The building looks spectacular at night, with light pouring through the glass blocks
3   The space is surrounded by natural light
4   Square openings are designed to breathe
5–7   Floor plans
8   View from first floor
9   Transparency of interior space allows connection to outside space
Photography: Makoto Yoshida

Davidson Residence

Evansville, Indiana, USA

VEAZEY PARROTT DURKIN & SHOULDERS

This distinctly modern 7200-square-foot (670-square-meter) residence stands in contrast to its setting in rural, southern Indiana. While revealing its apparent modern style, at the same time it reflects, through its form, the dignity of rural Indiana: its barns, silos and galvanized steel roofs. The primary design intention was to create an environment that expresses and supports the residents' artistic lifestyle, dreams, passions, and pastimes. The house functions as a getaway, a hideaway, a meditation retreat, an art gallery and an entertainment venue.

Site utilization includes a series of patios and decks designed to make it possible for the residents to interact with the pastoral Indiana countryside or to entertain friends. A special bonfire structure, complete with circular seating, is situated in the adjacent wooded area, visible from the pool structure and the wood deck that is attached to the house.

All systems in this residence incorporate high performance design, including energy recovery ventilators that contribute significantly to the dramatic energy efficiency of the house. High sidewall light slots, at the top of each of the silos, admit natural light in a very controlled and disciplined manner in order to highlight specific architectural features or the owners' artwork. The building is super insulated and indoor air quality is assured through use of fresh air intakes.

The residence was designed with efficient resource utilization in mind. Framing timber from nearby farms was utilized in portions of the roof structure. Hardwood flooring is also indigenous to rural southern Indiana. The indoor pool uses a bromine filtration system. Not only modern in design, this residence incorporates modern efficiency at all levels.

1

2

3

4

1 Entry detail at dusk
2 Entry at dusk
3 Exterior looking into pool area
4 Kitchen and dining, sunroom beyond
Photography: Nino G Cocchiarella

Deamer Residence

San Francisco, California, USA

MARK ENGLISH ARCHITECTS

The location is a typical San Francisco doublewide lot, 50 feet x 100 feet deep (15 x 30 meters), sloping down from the street to the east. To the north is Buena Vista Park, a heavily wooded hill. To the east, an inspiring view sweeps from downtown San Francisco, across the Berkeley hills and Mount Diablo to the nearby rolling hills of Diamond Heights. The house consists of 4000 square feet (372 square meters), over four levels.

The clients are a mature San Francisco couple who love to cook and travel. Like many San Franciscans, they soon found their favorite "village" upon arrival in this city of villages. For them, the Mission district is a perfect melding of Italian Hilltown and funky seaside town.

The prospect of substantially changing an existing old home is, in San Francisco, fraught with controversy and conflict. The architects' approach to the process was to keep the neighbors aware of design progress through a schedule of meetings, starting with a wine and cheese affair on one of the original crumbling wood roof terraces. In the end this strategy worked and all public hearings were avoided. The design process was unusual: after an initial meeting, the basic building program was quickly established; soon after, three different explorations were prepared in computer model form. An animation was produced using the favorite solution, and approval followed shortly thereafter.

The interior materials include 18-inch (46-centimeter) square French limestone floors with radiant heating, cork floor tiles, anigre cabinets and built-ins, waxed and hammered copper backsplash, custom stainless sink, marble countertops and Brazilian cherry butcher-block island top. The exterior is finished with natural copper sheathing at the façade and roof deck solid rail, brass trellis, China jade slate terrace paving, and Brazilian cherry deck pallet system.

1

2

1 View from kitchen toward the east
2 Kitchen built-in wall with niche
3 Exterior view of breakfast room from garden
4 South elevation
Photography: Michael O'Callahan

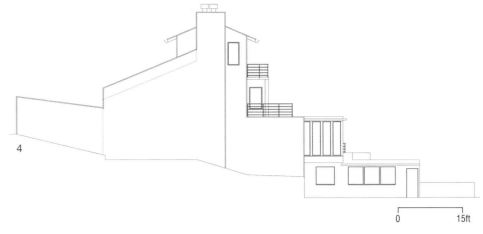

4

0   15ft

3

Denis House

Jehanster-Verviers, Belgium

DETHIER & ASSOCIÉS

According to the architects, the market for single-family housing in Belgium is virtually a monopoly of the "turnkey" companies. They believe the "four façade house" product is a caricature of traditional housing, where recycled bricks, concrete roofing tiles, and aged beams serve as pseudo turrets, skylights, and shutters that are screwed to the façades and decorated with lights. The more pollution the construction methods create, the more waste is created, to be buried under the buildings. The soil is waterproof, so waste water in the gutters causes overflows and floods during storms. There is little ecological thought about energy, or about adaptation to today's lifestyle.

The Denis house is the architects' alternative to the current situation. What is remarkable is that it obtained a building permit, proof that the local administration is supportive of alternative housing proposals. The idea is to offer a house that uses contemporary technologies—insulated glass, steel, roofing covered with vegetation, mechanical ventilation—to form economical housing, with a reduced surface area (1690 square feet/157 square meters), adapted to today's lifestyle and respectful of the environment.

To cut down on the habitable surfaces, traditional solutions, such as placing a bed in an alcove, were used. The master bedroom measures only 43 square feet (4 square meters) and looks like an extension of the library area; a sliding panel allows it to be partitioned off.

Entirely prefabricated, the building was assembled on limited foundations in the middle of an orchard. It forms a complete symbiosis with its environment and offers the occupants an intimate relationship with the natural world. The technical solutions are minimalist. To reduce the use of the mechanical ventilation system and avoid overheating, vines will grow over cables stretched in front of the sanded glass of the south façade. The shade from the leaves will make it possible in the summer to avoid overheating due to radiant energy from the sun and will also, because of the play of patches of light on the floor and the walls, provide continuous colored entertainment.

1 Northeast façade with nearby orchard
2 East façade reflects neighboring brick house
3 Ground floor plan
4 Mezzanine level plan

1

2

3

4

1	Entrance	6	Bathroom
2	Living	7	Laundry
3	Dining	8	Garage
4	Library	9	Study
5	Master bedroom	10	Bedroom

0   2m

5

5 West façade
6 Southwest façade shows artwork by Jean Gilbert through sandblasted glass
7 Living room
8 Southeast façade
9 Mezzanine level
Photography: Jean-Paul Legros

6

7

8

9

Du Plessis House

Paraty, Rio de Janeiro, Brazil

MARCIO KOGAN ARQUITETO

The house is located 9 miles (15 kilometers) from the historic city of Paraty, in Rio de Janeiro. The basic concept of the project was to explore architecture with a "double face": modern on the outside and conventional inside. Local regulations prescribed a tiled roof, which the architect integrated with his modernist approach.

The 4380-square-foot (407-square-meter) house is simply a large box faced with mineira stone (a stone from the Brazilian state of Minas Gerais), with a central external courtyard where four jaboticaba trees stand out from the swirled-pebbled paving. The exterior of the house, with its clay-tiled roof, looks modern, and fits in neatly with the requirements of the condominium estate in which it is located. Looking through the patio to the house reveals a more traditional interior design.

Four bedrooms and a small TV room are turned in to face the courtyard. All feature muxarabi wooden latticework from one end to another, which acts as a light filter. At night, seen from the courtyard when the lights of the rooms are on, this latticework covering is transformed into a glowing lantern.

The main room is turned out, facing the rear of the property, where the Atlantic rainforest begins. All the doors can be opened and the room joins a bamboo-covered terrace and the swimming pool beyond. An opening in the courtyard frames views of the estate's golf course.

1

1 Wooden latticework acts as a light filter to internal rooms
2 Detail of mineira stone exterior wall
3 Courtyard features four jaboticaba trees
4 Main room joins bamboo-ceilinged terrace and swimming pool
5 Front façade
Photography: Arnaldo Pappalardo

2

3

5

4

East St Kilda Residence

East St Kilda, Victoria, Australia

INARC ARCHITECTS

This expansive home was designed for a large and growing family devoted to the aesthetics of contemporary design. This duality of purpose between the modernist aesthetic and everyday family use is visible in the façades: the public face is a formal gray stone composition while the private face is a warmer timber-clad skin.

The totally transparent ground and first-floor windows are well disguised and hidden from the street, and give no indication as to the internal function, providing both anonymity and uniformity when the building is performing its extended family duties. These large areas of glass allow an intimate relationship with the landscape and garden vistas. Significant integration between the architecture and engineering was required to achieve the fenestration patterns on the first floor. Design features such as the highly rationalized external elevations, flat roof profiles, and minimal ground floor walls required the integration of innovative structural solutions.

The ground floor provides a public forum as well as a family living domain. Due to the flatness of the site and the lack of distant views, internal axes are introduced to control the sight lines within the property and to give focus at the end of long hallways.

The study has direct access to the entry for the reception of visitors, as well as a northern outlook onto a private courtyard garden. Beyond the study is the guest suite with its own bathroom and dressing area. Similar to the study, it is discreetly removed from the family living and bedroom areas, and has its own private outlook to the rear garden.

A large sitting area and an adjacent dining area can be divided or opened up by panels that slide back into nib walls. Large sliding glass doors allow these spaces to spill out onto the courtyards and gardens.

The kitchen opens onto its own courtyard at the front of the house, which in turn acts as an informal outdoor eating area as well as a play area for younger children with direct supervision from the kitchen.

The first floor accommodates all the bedrooms and bathrooms for the family. The children's bedrooms are arranged along the front elevation of the house, and are linked by an axial gallery that mirrors the main circulation axis on the ground floor. The main bedroom is a separate suite with an adjoining nursery.

1 Rear elevation detail
2 Front elevation
3 Pool rear elevation
4 Part rear elevation

1

2

3

4

5

6

7

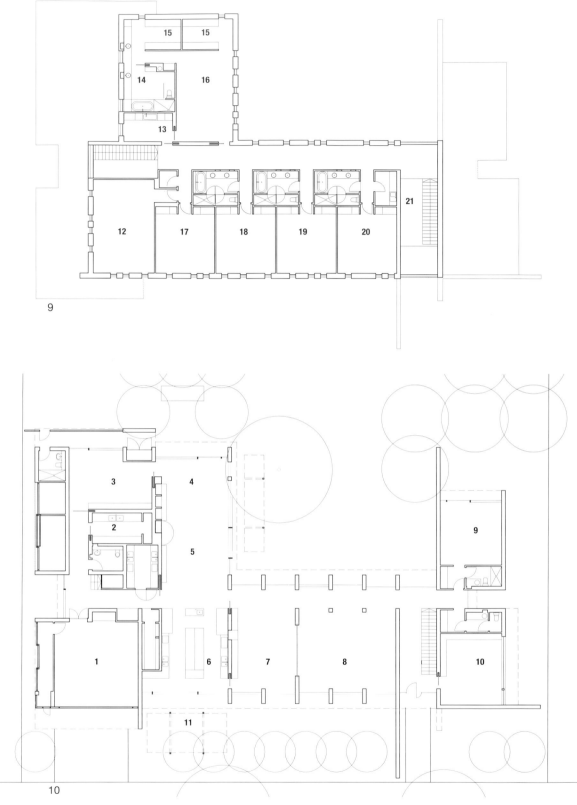

5   Rear elevation at night
6   Children's bedroom
7   Family room
8   Ensuite bathroom
9   First floor plan
10 Ground floor plan
Photography: Peter Clarke—Latitude Group

1	Garage	12	Playroom
2	Laundry	13	Nursery
3	Playroom	14	Ensuite
4	Living	15	Walk-in robe
5	Meals area	16	Bedroom 1
6	Kitchen	17	Bedroom 2
7	Dining	18	Bedroom 3
8	Sitting	19	Bedroom 4
9	Guest	20	Bedroom 5
10	Study	21	Void
11	Pergola		

Ecevit House

Potomac, Maryland, USA

MCINTURFF ARCHITECTS

Sited on a wooded slope adjacent to a meadow in Maryland's horse country, this house connects to the local farm vernacular through its simplicity of siting, form and detail. A straightforward L-shaped plan creates an entry court between the garage/service wing and the house proper, where a great room on the first floor is oriented to take advantage of views into a wooded ravine to the north. South light is brought into the house through selective fenestration toward the approach road and clerestory windows beneath shed roofs whose bracketed eaves support generous overhangs while referring to nearby barns. Finally, a screened porch pavilion flies off the body of the house projecting the eye, and the occupants, into the woods beyond.

1 Balcony detail
2 Front elevation
3 Screened porch

1

2

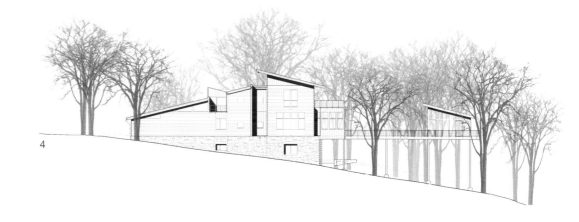

4

5

6

7

8

9

Photography: Julia Heine

Ecological House

Huizhou, Guang Dong Province, China

SHAONING CHEN, WANZHONG LIU; CSN STUDIO/BUILDING ENGINEERING DEPARTMENT SHENZHEN POLYTECHNIC

The owner and the architect worked together to achieve a type of "country style" for this house, in contrast to the stiffness often found in suburban or city houses. The emphasis was to be on comfort, with the incorporation of hand-made and natural materials in furniture and decoration where possible, in order to create a simple and elegant home.

The two-story, 11,840-square-foot (1100-square-meter) home comprises living areas on the ground floor, and sleeping and "rest" areas on the second floor. The two levels are connected by two sweeping curved staircases and an exterior staircase. The house's eclectic style is reflected in the surrounding pond, sloped roof, large doors and windows, and a traditional Chinese inner courtyard.

The ground-floor entrance hall is welcoming and warm with a teak front door, iron pendant lamps and a durable flagstone floor. This space leads to the large hallway with its log beams and wood frame roof presenting a rustic atmosphere. The living room features large doors and windows, ensuring copious natural light and ventilation. Sliding doors open onto the inner courtyard and exterior pond, drawing these "exernal" spaces inside and animating the interior space. A specially designed stone fireplace represents the simple architectural style of the house. The dining room is the focus of the house, with its ornate oak dining table again reflecting the "natural" style of the house.

The tea room is a traditional Chinese element, reflecting the local culture with its use of elm, rosewood and sandalwood. The exquisite inner yard is a further demonstration of the placement of conventional Chinese elements within a contemporary house.

The second-floor master bedroom is a study in space and luxury. Sunlight enters the room and reflects off the teak sloped ceiling and beams. A superbly handcrafted four-poster bed, together with an antique Chinese table, are eye-catching features of this room.

The designers were keen to include as many sustainable features as possible: large windows and sliding doors allow in light and ventilation and reduce reliance on mechanical air-conditioning; a roof-mounted solar system provides heat for the entire house. Natural, earth-colored materials were chosen to complement the "natural" atmosphere of the house, and include iron, teak, stone, terra cotta tile flooring, and red bricks.

1   Second-floor hallway
2   Living room
Opposite:
    Exterior at night

1

2

5

6

7

4   Entrance hall
5   Spacious master bedroom
6   Dining room
7   Tea room
Photography: Chensi/Pinshengxuan

Edgehill House

Toronto, Ontario, Canada

3RD UNCLE DESIGN

The Edgehill house is a private family residence located on the outskirts of Toronto. From the street its front elevation accentuates the horizontal plane, giving it the appearance of a low building. In contrast, the rear elevation gives the house a sense of verticality and transparency, expressed by the glass curtainwall.

The 11,000-square-foot (1022-square-meter) L-shaped plan maximizes its footprint on the property and divides the site into a series of interior and exterior spaces. The layout offers views of the garden from both sides of the house at the back and also maintains an intimate sense of scale. The centerpiece of the house is an open stair framed by a glass curtainwall on one side. In the evening the curtainwall illuminates the garden like a giant lantern.

On the main level, the central axis is a raised plinth clad in slabs of honed limestone. The grand room overlooks the front yard and the private garden behind the house through full-height windows. Access to the private garden is through an enormous glass pivot door. The dining area is staged on the raised plinth by the open stair. It overlooks the private garden and backyard with the swimming pool and hot tub through the full-height glass panels. Beyond the dining room is a sunken living area across from an open kitchen.

On the second level the children's bedrooms overlook the nearby park. The view is framed by a continuous horizontal strip window that runs along the front façade of the house. The master suite runs the length of the house on the upper level and is accessed through the intimate space of the wood-paneled library, overlooking the atrium. The curtainwall of textured glass spans the home office that is adjacent to the bedroom area, providing soft natural light.

The house is framed in steel and is clad in seamed copper, sappelli wood and light gray brick. Glass panels and curtainwall in both clear and translucent glass help dissolve the boundaries between exterior and interior and allow natural light to flow throughout the house. This is critical given the severe winter climate of Toronto.

Natural materials were used throughout. The limestone walls and flooring of the exterior extend through the interior spaces of the house, which incorporate radiant floor heating. The floors are a combination of hardwood and limestone.

1

2

3

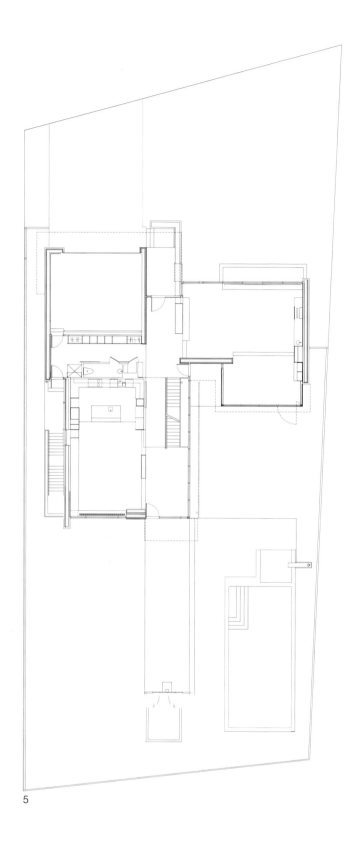

5

4

1 Grand stair is an open steel structure, with wood treads and a stainless steel handrail and glass guard
2 The illuminated screen and curtain wall composed of textured and transparent glass act as a lantern for the garden at night
3 The sunken grand room overlooks the front yard and private garden with full-height windows; the limestone wall and floor extends to the exterior of the building
4 Seen from the street, the overhanging flat room accentuates the horizontal, above the children's bedrooms; the entry is recessed
5 The plan is organized by the raised stone plinth that runs continuously through to the garden

Photography: Andrej Kopac

Ehrlich Residence

Santa Monica, California, USA

JOHN FRIEDMAN ALICE KIMM ARCHITECTS, INC.

The main challenge of this house was to resolve a contradiction between the clients' wishes and the site itself.
The clients wanted a sustainable house, optimally a south-facing structure with a thin profile to encourage maximum cross-breezes and sunlight penetration. At the same time, they wanted the living spaces to open onto the largest possible walled garden which, due to the city codes, was on the northeast side of the property.

The resulting first-floor plan shows an L-shaped series of living spaces wrapped around the garage and opening onto an L-shaped garden. On the southeast side, overhanging eaves block the summer sun, but allow the winter sun to heat up the concrete floor, which acts as a heat sink. The southwest façade is mostly solid to keep out the punishing western sun; the koi pond surrounding the living room cools the breezes that enter the main living spaces. The house is clad primarily with smooth-troweled plaster and shiplapped cement board, both in a subtle range of natural tones.

Strategies were developed to obtain the effects of a thin, south-facing house even though the main living areas face northeast. Hidden in the relatively strict orthogonal layout is a series of diagonals in plan and section that bring in wind and light from the south. A dramatic example is the monitor-like opening which can be seen on the second floor and whose eave faces due south. Created by dispersing the solid, service elements of the house to create a "diagonal void," during the winter it brings direct light to the furthest northern corner of the house. Just as importantly, this internal massing (as opposed to the more common external massing) creates an atrium space that not only contains the stair, but also vents the hot air of the house through a pair of motorized skylights in the roof.

The atrium has several roles beyond its sustainable function: its verticality contrasts with the compressed horizontality of much of the first floor, intensifying the interior's relationship with the garden. Its mixture of reflected and direct light tracks the sun during the day, and emits a lantern-like glow at night. The atrium also organizes the rooms on the second floor, particularly the master bedroom, which has an internal window that allows the clients to take in the ever-changing light in the double-height space. Situated to block noise from the busy boulevard, the master bathroom takes advantage of this quality with light from three different orientations.

1 Detail of main entrance
2 Entrance (southwest) façade at dusk
3 Garden façade and koi pond
4 Dining area with kitchen beyond
5 Master shower

1

2

3

4

5

6 Roof plan
7 Second floor plan
8 Ground floor and site plan
9 Foyer looking toward garden
10 Kitchen and garden
11 Garden (northeast) façade at dawn
12 Master bathtub
13 Stair and atrium
Photography: Benny Chan, Fotoworks

6

7

8

9

11

10

Ford Residence

Denver, Colorado, USA

HUTTON FORD ARCHITECTS

The homeowners, both architects, decided to expand their home, built in 1896, to accommodate a growing family. The program included renovating and expanding the kitchen, adding a family room and breakfast area and a second-floor master bedroom, to create a 2700-square-foot (250-square-meter) home.

The architecture of the addition is derivative of the original home while providing a modern sensibility; the goal was a seamless integration between old and new. Underlying organizing principles found in the 1896 architecture are incorporated into the addition: datums expressed as projected brick bands that organize windows and brick arches, masonry details, roof slopes and vertical proportions.

The contemporary interior utilizes structural elements and varied ceiling planes to define space and direct the eye. Low-cost materials such as gypsum board add to the simple expression. This honest expression is evident at the second-floor bedroom where the roof and structural forms define the character of the space. Six dormers overhead in the interior of the bedroom help to define various zones, including a natural canopy over the bed. The dormers also serve to provide a dynamic quality to the space with ceiling heights varying from 3 to 15 feet (1 to 4.5 meters). Paired structural columns help to subdivide the bedroom into distinct zones for sleeping and washing. The exterior wall is pushed and pulled to create areas for window seats at the first and second floor.

At the main level, the floor of the new family room is 16 inches (41 centimeters) lower than the existing main floor to provide an 11-foot (3.4-meter) ceiling. Soffits and arches are used to provide rhythm, define space and take the eye to the sandstone fireplace at the south wall. The roof and ceiling also step up at the fireplace to give a sense of visual lift and direct the eye upwards along the tapered lines of the fireplace, terminating in ridge skylights, which wash the sandstone in natural light. Full height windows frame the fireplace. Also at the south wall, the exterior Flemish bond brick with its recessed header pattern is continued inside and out to provide color and texture. The structural columns between the family room and the kitchen areas create an arched entry feature and provide rhythm and a visual break at the point where the floor level changes.

2

3

1   View of family room addition
2   Exterior view of fireplace at addition
3   Exterior view of addition

4 Second floor plan
5 First floor plan
6 Master bathroom addition
7 Master bedroom addition, looking south
8 View from renovated kitchen into addition
9 View of renovated portion of original kitchen
Photography: Ron Johnson (1,7–9); Jackie Shumaker (2,3,6)

126

1	Porch/entry	11	Sun porch
2	Foyer	12	Old master bedroom
3	Living room	13	Bedroom
4	Dining room	14	Library
5	Renovated kitchen	15	Bathroom
6	Toilet	16	Master bedroom
7	Kitchen	17	Her walk-in robe
8	Breakfast area	18	His walk-in robe
9	Family room	19	Master bathroom
10	Deck	20	Family room (below)

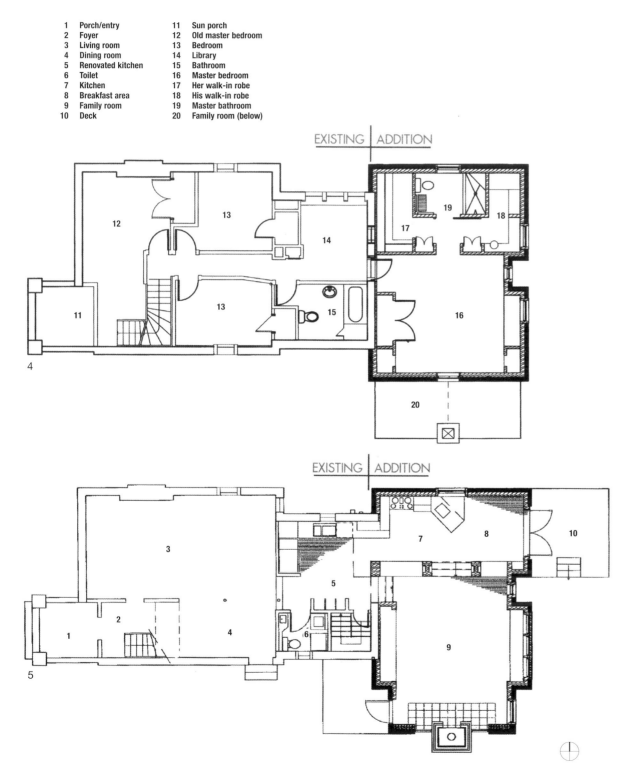

Fritz Residence

Palm Desert, California, USA

OJMR ARCHITECTS

The house is located on a flat, irregularly shaped lot at the end of a cul-de-sac. The neighborhood contains a variety of styles and references to the preferred typical suburban desert subdivision architecture.

The 2600-square-foot (242-square-meter) house was designed for a retired couple with the need for guest bedroom suites and a large communal space for the living, dining, and kitchen areas.

To achieve a feeling of "simplicity" within conventional means, it was decided that planning and construction must be straightforward, and the character of the house reflect a strategy of enclosure and openness focused toward the main outdoor space. Two simple volumes are connected together to define a corner, with one wing containing the guest bedrooms, and the other containing the master suite. The two wings are connected at the main living, dining, and kitchen space.

Hallways are located along the east and south sides of the two wings and help to define the laterally situated rooms, which can be closed off from the circulation zone with large sliding walls. The rooms all access the outdoor pool/courtyard space from large sliding glass walls.

Materials incorporated in this project include exposed concrete block walls, natural stone veneer walls, plaster over wood framing, concrete floors, walnut cabinetry, Gascogne blue limestone floors in bathrooms, translucent glass panels, Montauk black marble counters in the kitchen, and Venetino white marble countertops in the bathroom and on the kitchen island.

1

1   The drive-up elevation shows deep eaves for shade and drama
2   This "New-Century Modernist" house reflects the tenets of classic desert Modernism
3   Two wings meet at public areas of kitchen and living room

2

4

4 Mix of architect-designed furniture and vintage Danish Modern combine in the living room
5 Rooms are separated by moving lateral walls
6 Floor plan shows fluid organization of the house
7 Master bath is a layered play of transparency and reflection
Photography: Ciro Coelho

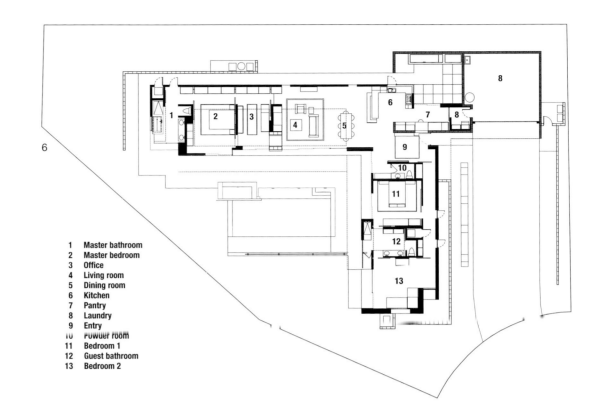

6

1 Master bathroom
2 Master bedroom
3 Office
4 Living room
5 Dining room
6 Kitchen
7 Pantry
8 Laundry
9 Entry
10 Powder room
11 Bedroom 1
12 Guest bathroom
13 Bedroom 2

5

7

Gibbeson House

Surry Hills, New South Wales, Australia

STANIC HARDING PTY LTD

The architects' brief was to breathe new life into a poorly built mid-1980s three-level townhouse. The solution resulted in a total strip-out of all levels, a new rear façade, the refurbishment of an existing courtyard, which extends into the interior space, and the inclusion of a pond as a focus to all levels.

The lower level is now a garage, TV/guest room and courtyard; the middle level includes kitchen, dining, living and balcony space, and the upper level accommodates bedrooms, study, and bathrooms. The house is small (1710 square feet/159 square meters) so all elements are carefully proportioned and placed. Major elements float and slip above the ground plane, giving a sense of extended space.

To facilitate entry of light and air movement a slice is made across each floor level, culminating in a new ventilated skylight. An aluminum slatted floor bridges the slice at each level and helps define either a change in level or function. Emphasis is placed on a series of reflected and extended views to add richness to this small house. Open stairs, slatted floors, glass, considered openings, frames, and worked edges assist in enriching these vistas.

All three interior levels are connected to the exterior court. A colored concrete slab extends the interior into the courtyard and vice versa. An ornamental pond with a "floating" pebble-clad screen is the focus of this exterior space and can be seen from all three levels of the house. The scheme works with the existing alignments and levels while presenting a more transparent face to the north and the courtyard.

On the lowest level the courtyard and interior fuse with various floor and wall elements. The middle level offers a transitional balcony space complete with an indoor/outdoor joinery element from which to view the courtyard. The top level absorbs the existing balcony and presents a full-height louvered window, which allows long views as well as focusing on the rear courtyard. Steel-framed doors are designed to fold open to directly connect both realms. Joinery, floor plates, and stairs float above the floor plane and slip over each other to extend space and give the house a calm tension.

1 Lower level TV/guest room viewed from courtyard with garage beyond
2 Night view showing multilayered courtyard façade
3 Exposed steel beam to edge of slatted floor above living room

1

2

1 Courtyard
2 TV space
3 Garage
4 Guest WC
5 Driveway
6 Deck
7 Living
8 Dining
9 Kitchen
10 Bedroom
11 Robe
12 Bathroom
13 Study

10

11

4   Upper level floor plan
5   Entry level floor plan
6   Courtyard level floor plan
7   Stairwell offers visual connection to all internal levels and exterior
8   Water feature at end wall of courtyard
9   Middle level view looking to courtyard from living/dining area
10 Joinery wall allows view to skylit stairwell from main bedroom
11 Aluminum-clad rear façade showing indoor/outdoor connection
Photography: Paul Gosney

Grosse Pointe Residence

Grosse Pointe, Michigan, USA

MCINTOSH PORIS ASSOCIATES

The original house was built in 1928 by Smith Hynchman and Grylls on a 5-acre (2-hectare) lot in Grosse Pointe Farms. Two wings were added to the existing three-story brick house, which accommodates a great room, dining room, ballroom, sitting room, conservatory, ladies' lounge, men's library with bar and smoking porch, a professional catering kitchen, master bedroom suite with his-and-hers bathrooms and walk-in closets, and guest rooms.

The clients wished to completely renovate and add to their existing French Eclectic style home to better fit with their current lifestyle. They often entertain and hold fundraising events for as many as 1000 people. The task was to design the house to function both as a home and as a small art institution. Further, the design needed to match the quality and detail of their collection of French art, fixtures, and furnishings while at the same time illuminating and protecting them from environmental deterioration.

Taking cues from the original house, the architects placed the additions symmetrically at each end of the existing main structure. These "pavilion"-like structures both extend and sit forward from the original house, allowing for the creation of a large limestone terrace facing Lake St. Clair. One pavilion functions as a great room off the kitchen while the other is a ballroom for entertaining. Galleries connect the pavilions back to the original house, and provide access to additional new spaces, including an expanded kitchen, pantry and serving areas, a bar room, smoking porch, oval ante-room, bathrooms, and catering kitchen on the more formal end of the house. The second floor was completely reworked to create a new master suite, guest rooms, exercise, and other ancillary spaces.

All existing interior spaces have been remodeled using both new and antique architectural and decorative detailing in matching brick, limestone, and wrought iron. To formalize the overall appearance of the structure, the architects added classical limestone detailing and a columned central façade to the original structure.

The new great room and ballroom spaces feature over-scaled, custom Rumford fireplaces. The "his" and "hers" master bathrooms feature a book-matched and running pattern of African onyx. While classic in language, the house provided the architects an opportunity to reinvent the exquisite detailing and architectural language of another era while at the same time creating a house that functions for the unique requirements of today.

1 Sprawling rooms hold 1000 people at charity events
2 Kitchen is equipped for professional caterers
3 Two wings are added onto the existing central volume
4 The house is replete with French antiques and art
5 A series of oculi enhance the formal ballroom
Photography: Laszlo Regos (1,4,5); Beth Singer (2); Jeff Garland (3)

1

2

3

4

5

Haus Martin

San Francisco, California, USA

CCS ARCHITECTURE

This new single-family house, located in the Buena Vista Park district of San Francisco, replaces an existing home with the same footprint and number of stories. In addition to the client's program, the house is designed to respond to two contextual influences: the excellent views of the park to the east and of the ocean to the west, plus the richly ornate façades of the adjacent neighbors. The existing house, which was demolished, was a small home with little distinction wedged between a flamboyant turn-of-the-century Victorian and an elaborate 1920's Craftsman-style mansion.

The intent was to create a façade that would equate to the adjacent façades in intensity, materiality, and interest, yet be purely modern. This goal was merged with maximizing the width of the windows to create a horizontal pan of the dramatic views. The recessed garage creates a vestibule where one enters the house to the right. Slats of stained cedar over dark blue plywood are the primary cladding to the front, while cement plaster wraps the sides and rear of the building. Fronting the entry area, the slats extend in front of a full-height window, which admits filtered light.

The two-level plan is about clever restraint and unorthodox minimalism. The first floor accommodates sleeping, and the clients' wardrobe in an open plan without doors that leads to the deck and views to the west. The master bathroom is the only one in the house, with a WC room that allows for access from two sides.

The second floor is for cooking, eating, and living; the rooms are arranged in an axial diagonal that terminates at a free-hanging fireplace called a "fire-orb". This diagonal axis is oriented toward views of the Pacific Ocean to the west, and over Cole Valley and the Sunset District. The kitchen cabinets and appliances are entirely contained within a stainless steel assemblage that extends to become the walnut dining table—with an overall length of 30 feet (9 meters).

Primary interior materials are restrained, yet expressive: white walls create a sharp and neutral background for the walnut and stainless steel.

1 Front elevation
2 Design sketch
3 Façade at dusk
4 Front window admits filtered light
5 Bookshelf/translucent stair guardrail

1

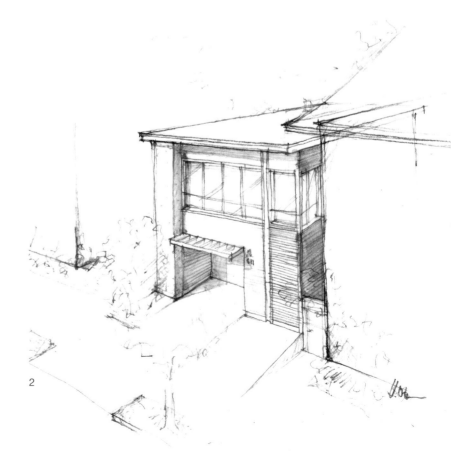

2

3

4

5

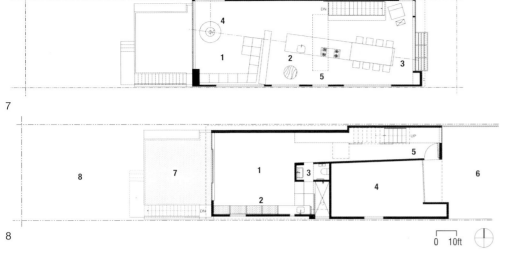

1 Living
2 Kitchen
3 Dining
4 Fire orb
5 Skylight

7

1 Bedroom
2 Closets
3 Bathroom
4 Garage
5 Entry
6 Driveway
7 Deck
8 Rear yard

8

0   10ft

6   Cabinets and appliances housed within
    stainless steel assemblage
7   Second floor plan
8   First floor plan
9   Fire orb
10 Sleeping level with open plan
11 Walnut dining table
Photography: Tim Griffith

9

10

11

Hope Ranch Residence

Santa Barbara, California, USA

SHUBIN + DONALDSON ARCHITECTS, ADLER ARQUITECTOS

Hope Ranch is a former working ranch that has been subdivided into equestrian oriented, mostly Western ranch-style estates.

This project included the new construction of a 7500-square-foot (697-square-meter) primary residence and a 3000-square-foot (280-square-meter) pool structure for the client and his family. A "contemporary house with a Mexican flavor" is what the art-collecting client requested. The architects responded with a contextual mélange of multiple orthogonal volumes that reflect a refined Mexican spirit in shape and material. The solidity of forms on one side of the home speaks to the Mexican flavor of the structure, while the abundance of glazing on the other side relates to the physical context of the coastal site.

The rough plaster of the 18-inch-thick (45-centimeter) walls—the same finish seen often in Mexico—adds texture and depth, and softens the monumentality of the forms. Although in the vein of Mexican architecture, this home departs in the choice of color, with a decidedly neutral, earthy pigment. Contrasting with the rough forms is the limestone-clad entry volume that appears to slice through the plaster volumes. The entry separates the home's public and private spaces.

Responding to the site, the architects created a constant interplay between indoor and outdoor in a continual effort to frame views and compose angles. Upon entering the building, beyond the play of forms, is the surprise view through the entry toward the negative-edge reflecting pool and out to the ocean beyond. Large, floor-to-ceiling windows wrap around a fountain, which also brings light into the home. One can go from the living room to the dining room across the stepping stones in the central reflecting pool.

An indoor swimming pool is accessed down the stairs from the master suite through a curved corridor that sports a rare hint of vibrant color. A deep orange curving corridor and sparkling blue wall in the pool house are a nod to the traditional Mexican palette. Three skylights punctuate the space that houses a 60-foot-long (18-meter) lap pool.

The owners wanted the house to have public spaces for social events. The dramatic open foyer and entry create a seamless experience for visitors as they journey from exterior to interior. Exterior limestone is repeated in the flooring, with contrasting darker limestone stripes echoing the ceiling articulation. Mexican tzalam wood is used for the custom-made doors, the spectacular interior bridge, and the interior wood floors.

1 Curved orange wall leads to indoor pool house
2 Geometric groupings define the home
3 Lighting, glass, and water heighten the drama

1

2

5

4

6

7

4 Cool limestone lines the master bath
5 Open kitchen is in keeping with modern flow of spaces
6 Internal bridge is made from Mexican tzalam wood
7 Blue of the pool house is a nod to the traditional Mexican color palette
Photography: Ciro Coelho

House in Berkeley

Berkeley, California, USA

MOORE RUBLE YUDELL

The clients' brief was for a house that was quiet and elemental, but rich with experiences. When they lost their original house to the Oakland/Berkeley fire in 1991, some remnants of the garden and fountains survived. Seeking a sense of continuity, these elements were integrated into the site plan and geometry of the new house. While the old house was well proportioned, it had stood somewhat independent of the site. The new 3910-square-foot (363-square-meter) house is shaped to engage the terraced landscape.

A bridge over the entryway frames the Golden Gate Bridge while a central tower anchors the house to its site. The gateway view begins a sequence of connections to close and borrowed landscape.

The secluded garden side of the house is developed as a set of built elements linking the hillside terraces. Circulation is through outside stairs and courts or through a choreographed internal sequence. The calm of quietly proportioned rooms contrasts the complexity of movement. Daylight is carefully washed against gallery walls, which support a vibrant contemporary collection.

The second floor serves as a retreat for the parents. Bedroom, bath, and library are linked "en suite" by a generous porch shading western sun and framing views to the Bay. This sequence is connected by a bridge to one son's "tower" pavilion bedroom, in contrast to the other's "garden" pavilion at the lowest level.

The elemental forms of the whole animate the site and heighten the exploration of the land and views. The movement from garden to sky reveals a diversity of experiences and emotions.

1 Second-story bridge between guest wing and
   master bedroom porch
2 Doors from dining area to terraced garden
3 Doors to kitchen garden
4 Double-height living room designed to
   accommodate large paintings
5 Rear elevation and terraced garden
Photography: Kim Zwarts

1

2

3

4

5

House C

Lomas de Chapultepec, Mexico City, Mexico

TALLER DE ENRIQUE NORTEN ARQUITECTOS, SC (TEN ARQUITECTOS)

House C is situated on a sloped site of approximately 4304 square feet (400 square meters), in Mexico City's exclusive Lomas de Chapultepec neighborhood.

Because of the high exposure of its corner site, the architects decided on an L-shaped plan, which opens up to the north, as the optimum way of providing the house with the most privacy from the street. The L-shaped plan, coupled with the house's high wall enclosure, make the indoor–outdoor spaces the central focus of the house

The double-height main entrance runs through the stairs and weaves through the primary living space and bedrooms above. The primary living room, dining room and indoor–outdoor spaces are located on the middle floor. They are linked to the bedrooms and family room above, and to the library and stone-paved courtyard below, by stairs on the east side of the house. The ground floor also contains the house's six-car garage.

Throughout the house is a playful collage of space and view, granted further complexity and richness by the continuity of materials from the inside to outside, which blurs the distinction between interior and exterior conditions. The collage effect culminates in the top-floor family room, which offers expansive views of the interior. From here, the double heights of the ground floor library and the living room are woven together with the skyline, granting the distant view a new immediacy.

1 View through house from family room
2 Main entrance
3 Rear patio
4 Second level family room
5 View through house from library
Photography: Luis Gordoa

1

2

3

4

5

House Corthout

Schilde, Belgium

CLAIRE BATAILLE & PAUL IBENS IN COLLABORATION WITH ARCHITECT LIEVEN LANGOHR

The client wanted a house with a close relationship to its surroundings. The design solution was to bring the outdoors in, by using as much glass as possible. An exterior glass wall creates an intimate inner garden and at the same time provides necessary privacy. The living rooms are situated to the south with an overall view of the garden; the bedrooms are situated to the north and the front of the house.

In the center of the 4305-square-foot (400-square-meter) house is a closed courtyard, which again allows as much daylight as possible to enter and repeats the contact with nature from wherever one looks. The symmetry of the courtyard is repeated outside to form a terrace next to the living room. As the courtyard brings nature inside, the terrace gives the impression that living continues outside.

Transparency is achieved with the use of a prefabricated glass and steel structure, with Eternit cement panels placed on a concrete base. Wooden floors and white-painted walls complete the basic palette.

1   View of garden from side of house
2   Guest room
3   Rear of house
4   Living room
Photography: Jean-Luc Laloux

1

2

3

4

House in Delray Beach

Delray Beach, Florida, USA

ANTHONY AMES ARCHITECT

The site is located on Highway A1A, opposite to the beach, which runs north–south. Access to the site is from a residential street perpendicular to the highway that borders the site to the south.

The ocean's edge, the beach, the linear vegetation separating it from the highway, the highway itself, and the edge of the site, are all factors in the layered situation and contribute to an evident frontality. The main block of the house fronts the road and everything else. The 3200-square-foot (297-square-meter) house is elevated on columns, presenting a façade that overlooks the road toward the beach and the ocean beyond. The major spaces—living, dining, master bedroom, and a small floating office—are open to this vista and are contained in the poured-in-place concrete shell. The façade is of white ceramic tile.

Perpendicular to this main block is an "L" that contains the secondary spaces: a garage at ground level, the second bedroom on the first level, and the master bath suite on the second level. This wing addresses a courtyard formed by its adjacency to the main block of the house. It is made of concrete block with a white stucco finish for emphasis.

Further back on the site a 790-square-foot (73-square-meter) guesthouse helps formalize the space and creates a symmetry with the "L" that defines the entry to the site from the residential street. It is also constructed of concrete block with a white stucco finish. There is a formal court and a service court—the former contains a whirlpool and a lap pool that slides under the elevated main block of the house and the latter contains a car park and a basketball court that address the guesthouse.

Varying spatial experiences that include glazed, light-filled, double-height spaces; enclosed, contained idealized rooms; slots of space and cozy personal places of repose, are accessed by various stairs, hallways, bridges and ladders. An active lifestyle is enhanced and encouraged by a "promenade architectural" that commences at the ground level next to the pool and culminates on the roof terrace with a view of the ocean.

1

2

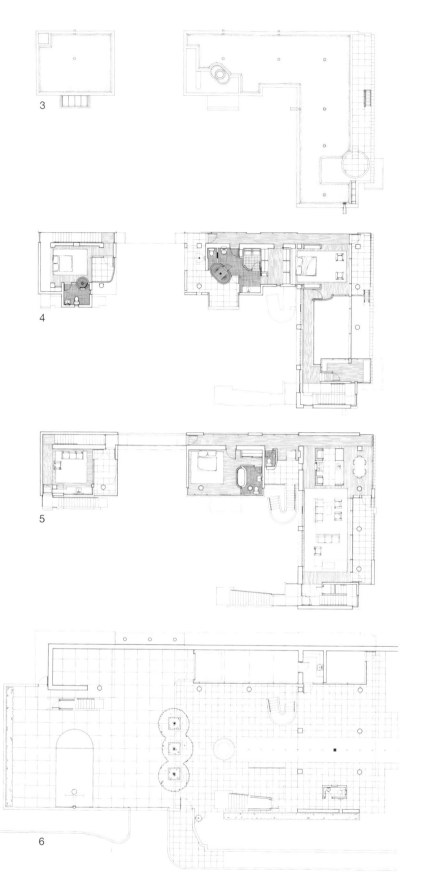

3

4

5

6

7

8

Photography: Scott Frances

10

11

House for GOA

Sunshine Coast, Queensland, Australia

BLIGH VOLLER NIELD PTY LTD

The brief for this holiday home on Australia's Sunshine Coast called for a contemporary interpretation of traditional tropical Pacific architecture. The clients were keen to explore and exploit the characteristics offered by the contemporary and traditional tropical architecture of Southeast Asia and sub-tropical Australia in a local setting.

The design responds to the existing house's footprint and fan-shaped site in a manner that maximises site usage. The narrow street frontage opens out to the rear of the site, allowing the design to focus on the view over the water beyond. Entering the house through the street-side gatehouse and confined entry corridor, the drama of the open living spaces and canal view is concealed from the street. The U-shaped plan enhances the sense of privacy from the street and neighbors, allowing the creation of a central courtyard space that links the living spaces at ground level. This roofed courtyard with associated swimming pool and pond creates a focal point for the house over both levels, drawing the eye out to the water beyond.

The upper-floor bedrooms are oriented around a generous central stair void with an associated skylight through which natural light filters into the deeper parts of the house. From the upper-floor bedrooms, large opening glass doors direct the view out over the crafted shingled roof of the arcaded court below.

The orientation of the site toward the canal demanded a strong response to the impact of the western sun. The use of deep outdoor rooms (Lanai and Bale) to the west combined with operable sunshading blinds, shutters, and screens has ensured both shading and privacy.

The use of timber, stone, glass, copper, bamboo, and natural textiles has resulted in a highly tactile and relaxed house, ideal for coastal living.

The 6240-square-foot (580-square-meter) building maximises site usage without compromising on the desired "tropical" quality within the house. This requirement of the client to feel "exposed to the elements" has been enhanced by a careful integration of dense landscaping, water features, diffused skylights, and natural materials.

1 Master bathroom
2 Bale from dining and kitchen areas
3 The house sits on the edge of a small private beach

1

2

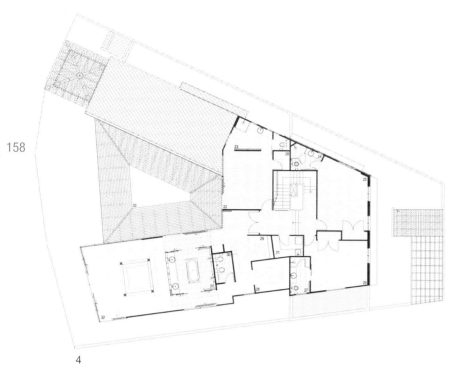

4

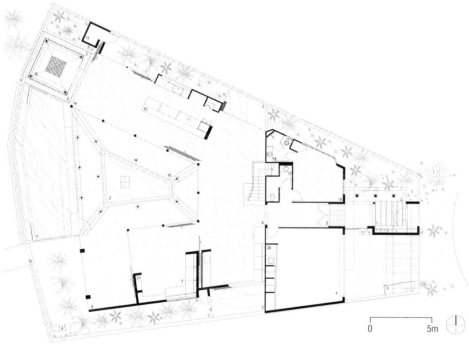

5

0   5m

6

1	Gatehouse	8	Lanai	15	Kitchen	22	Bedroom 4	29	Study
2	Pond	9	Outdoor shower	16	Arcaded court	23	Bathroom 4	30	WC
3	Storage	10	Jetty	17	Powder room	24	Bathroom 2	31	Ensuite
4	Garage	11	Pool	18	Bathroom 1	25	Bedroom 2	32	Master bedroom
5	Entry	12	Bale	19	Bedroom 1	26	Bedroom 3	33	Void
6	Hall	13	Pool equipment	20	Laundry	27	Bathroom 3	34	Canal
7	Lounge	14	Dining	21	Fireplace	28	Walk-in robe		

7

8

4 Upper level floor plan
5 Lower level floor plan
6 Kitchen with courtyard beyond
7 A crafted timber courtyard roof surrounds the central reflecting
  pond with views across the courtyard to the lounge and Lanai
8 Entry hall with stair to upper levels
Photography: David Sandison

House in Lake Forest

Lake Forest, Illinois, USA

STUART COHEN & JULIE HACKER

Built on a wooded site that backs onto a wetland nature preserve, this house offered the opportunity for both seclusion and beautiful views. A clearing was carved out of the forest to afford a lawn behind the informal living areas and space for a small formal kitchen garden at the side of the garage. The house is approached by a winding drive that terminates in an automobile turnaround. A short driveway connects the front to the side-facing attached garages.

The exterior of the house is sheathed in cedar shingles with white painted windows and trim. The roof is also cedar singles. The house is entered from a single-story front porch that stretches the full length of the living room. Immediately to the east of the entry porch and also facing the front is the service entrance, which is separated from the entry court by a full-height garden wall. Inside the entry hall the main stair rises up through the house, first to a mezzanine overlooking the two-story living room with its vaulted ceiling, then continuing up to the owner's home office in the house's tower.

The living room and dining room are a single space differentiated by a change in ceiling height. The dining room opens through French doors to a covered back porch. The kitchen, breakfast bay, and family room open to one another, forming a single informal living space across the back of the house. The kitchen and family room cabinetry and fireplace mantel are all made from figured maple. On the second floor the main bedrooms are reached from the mezzanine that overlooks the living room. The master suite stretches across the back of the house with the sleeping room opening to a roof deck over the breakfast room. From the master bathroom, the tub, shower stall and toilet all face out with views of forest landscape.

1 Living room
2 Front façade

1

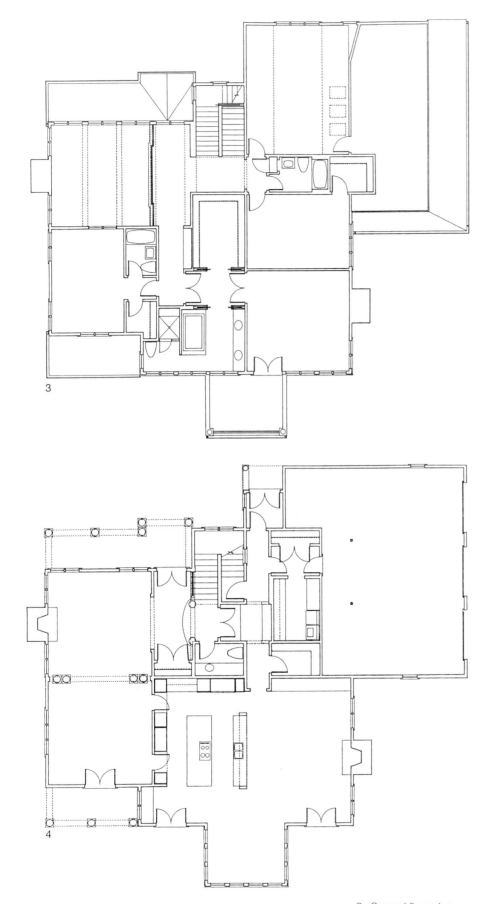

3

4

5

6

3   Second floor plan
4   First floor plan
5   Kitchen
6   Master bathroom
7   Living room looking toward dining room
Photography: Jon Miller/Hedrich-Blessing

House in Pacific Palisades

Pacific Palisades, California, USA

MOORE RUBLE YUDELL

The clients wanted a house that was both economical and expressive. They sought the playful and sensuous nature of curved forms, both because of the wife's background as a modern dancer and for their energetic young sons. The house combines the economies of large, simply enclosed loft spaces with the interior organization of a curved spine. The metaphor of a body in motion is present both in concept and in experience. Living spaces are organized along the spine and reach out into the landscape as limbs defining and flowing into intimate outdoor spaces.

The house is placed along the narrow buildable portion of the lot. Entry is celebrated at the beginning of the spine. One slips through spaces that contract and expand vertically. The spine of the house terminates in a small garden sheltered by a tree canopy: a space of quiet and contemplation completing the mind/body duality.

The large central gallery acts as the focus of activity, connecting spaces and paths vertically and linking horizontally to hillside and ocean-side gardens. Upstairs, the spine becomes a bridge between the children's and the parents' bedrooms. The bridge doubles as bench and library. A small study is tucked into a bay, which watches over the entry, and a tower study completes the vertical choreography, reaching up for light and views to the ocean and city.

The geometries and choreography of this house transform a simple loft typology into a richly woven hierarchy of places to move through and inhabit.

1 View of Pacific Ocean from terrace
2 Nestled into a steep hillside site, view of rear of house and ocean beyond
3 Double-height dining area connects to both view terrace and outdoor garden

1

2

4 Entry court
5 Staircase spills into foyer
6 Living space wraps around view terrace
7 Master bath windows offer views to hills
8 Terrace adjacent to living spaces
9 Second floor plan
10 Ground floor plan
Photography: Kim Zwarts

4

5

6

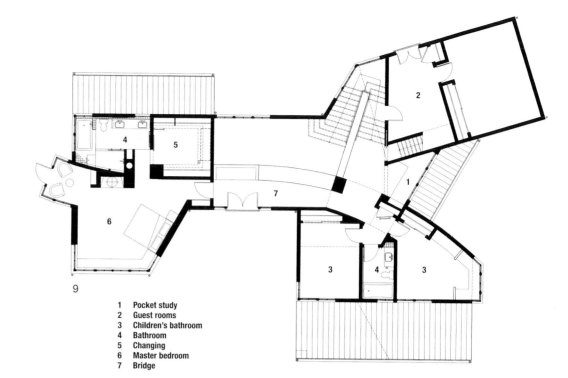

9

1 Pocket study
2 Guest rooms
3 Children's bathroom
4 Bathroom
5 Changing
6 Master bedroom
7 Bridge

7

8

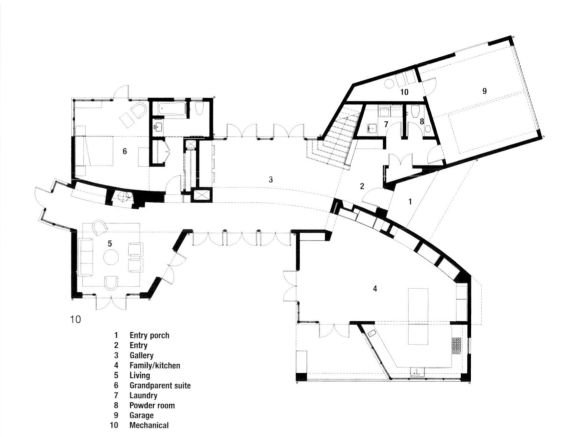

10

1 Entry porch
2 Entry
3 Gallery
4 Family/kitchen
5 Living
6 Grandparent suite
7 Laundry
8 Powder room
9 Garage
10 Mechanical

House of Silence

Finland

JUHANI PALLASMAA ARCHITECTS

This vacation house and sauna, on an exceptionally beautiful lakeside site, was designed as a retreat for the family and guests of a musician and a director of an art center in Eastern Finland.

The house proper contains an ample living room, double-height library, kitchen–dining area, bathroom and service facilities on the ground level, and three bedrooms upstairs along a suspended corridor which terminates in a screened and skylit porch above the terrace of the main floor.

The sauna structure contains a skylit dressing room with a fireplace and kitchenette, sauna and shower room. The partly covered outdoor area toward the house is used to store firewood, and the terrace in the opposite end contains a wood-lined Japanese bath tub sunk into the floor. The ensemble is completed by a wooden pier, a service building painted black in the middle of a group of boulders, and a future teahouse on top of the rocky hill behind the house proper.

The buildings with their multitude of openings are conceived to orchestrate views and light, like a cinematic montage: as the concrete wall of the sauna pushes into the ground, the skylight through the turf roof allows a view of the tree tops; the glass roof above the staircase allows views of the forest behind.

The structure is a combination of steel tube columns and wood structures. The exterior of the house is treated with tar, matched with the orange color of pine bark; the sauna is tarred black to deepen the impression of earth and shadow. The interior surfaces of the house are stained bone white; the sauna interiors are entirely of untreated red alder. All building components with the exception of hinges and door pulls were custom-made by local carpenters.

The project was given its name, House of Silence, in the course of the construction as it became evident that the interplay of nature and architecture enabled the dweller to recover the precious silence of his/her soul.

1

2

1 Western tip of the house
2 Summer house seen from the shore line
3 Summer house seen from arrival
4 Site plan
5 Sauna and summer house seen from the pier

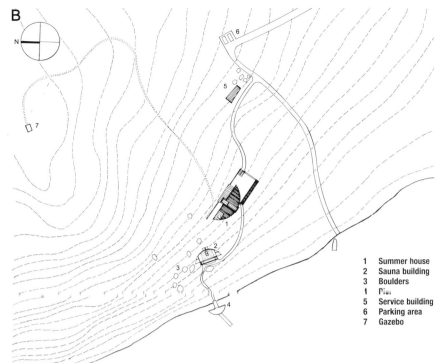

B

N

1 Summer house
2 Sauna building
3 Boulders
4 Pier
5 Service building
6 Parking area
7 Gazebo

3

4

5

170

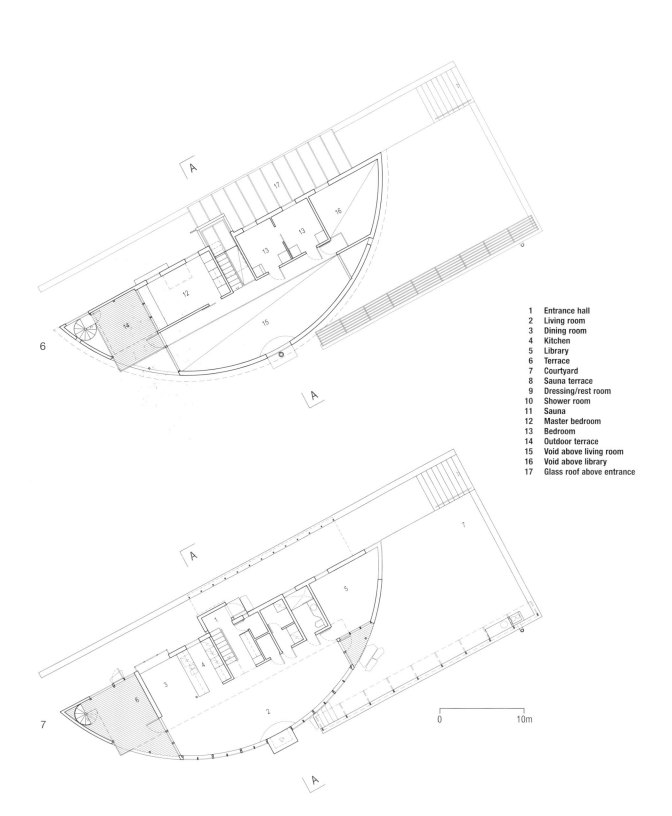

1 Entrance hall
2 Living room
3 Dining room
4 Kitchen
5 Library
6 Terrace
7 Courtyard
8 Sauna terrace
9 Dressing/rest room
10 Shower room
11 Sauna
12 Master bedroom
13 Bedroom
14 Outdoor terrace
15 Void above living room
16 Void above library
17 Glass roof above entrance

0   10m

8

9

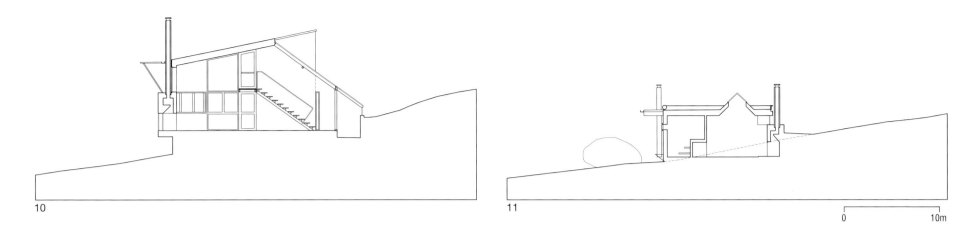

10

11

0   10m

12

House in Sorocaba

Sorocaba, São Paulo, Brazil

GERSON CASTELO BRANCO

Designed for a couple with two teenage children, the 10,760-square-foot (1000-square-meter) house offers generous spaces that open to the beautiful sunsets in the afternoon. On the narrower side of the lot, on opposite sides, are both the living and the service areas. The large front façade faces the city. On the lower floor the living area is integrated with the kitchen, the swimming pool, the garage and the service center. The mezzanine/library, study, four bedrooms and bathrooms, and the verandas are located on the second floor.

A large glass roof was created and installed, to give the house natural illumination. The main floor of the house features heating beneath the wood floor. Marble for the bathrooms and tiles in the kitchen and service areas complete the materials. A wood and steel sculpture/stair is a further feature of the interior architecture.

The interior decoration was completed by the client. The architect's only concern was that the furniture was placed to complement the main element of the architecture—the wall panels, which were deliberately left bare.

1

2

3

1 Façade detail
2 Main entry
3 Detail of wall panel
4 Main façade looking west

4

174

6

5

7

8

9

House in Woodside

Woodside, California, USA

MOORE RUBLE YUDELL

By using geometries that are curvilinear in plan and section, the Moore Ruble Yudell design team of Buzz Yudell and Mario Violich strove to express a sculptural quality to the residential design of this house in Woodside, California. As the building's mass rises, sloping roof planes of blue slate mimic the topography and integrate with adjacent hardscape materials. An "auto court" of decomposed granite leads through a formal entry to a gallery of the main residence. This gallery is the central organizational spine for the house, from which rooms and courtyards "saddlebag", and interplay with blue slate patios and water elements. Light monitors and loft rooms bring indirect light into the home. Intensely pigmented integral-colored plaster walls, monumental scale of openings and courtyards reflect the client's memories of childhood of colonial Guadalajara, Mexico, reinterpreted in a contemporary context.

Local design review authorities enforced scenic view corridors, restricting the building's height and mass to two narrow 60 x 100-foot (18 x 30-meter) envelopes on the client's 5-acre (2-hectare) site. The architects created an urban solution in a rural location, emphasizing a strong connection between earth and sky.

Landscape elements connect the main house and guest cottage: a citrus grove, meadow, and two allées that "bookend" the buildings. A ribbon-like pathway follows the rolling topography, threading through the architecture and landscape.

1

1 Pool terrace and courtyard with living room beyond
2 Landmark California live oak tree at auto court
3 Central gallery at entry with living spaces beyond

2

3

4

4 Main courtyard with views to central
  gallery, family and living rooms
5 Living room with view to pool terrace
  beyond
6 Pool terrace at living room
7 Second floor plan
8 Ground floor plan
9 Master bedroom and south terrace
Photography: Art Gray

5

6

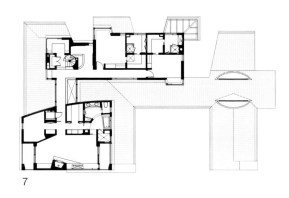

7

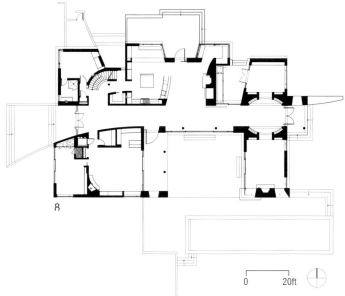

8

0   20ft

9

Iporanga House

Iporanga Beach, São Paulo, Brazil

SANDRA PICCIOTTO ARCHITECTURE AND INTERIORS

Young and demanding clients wanted a stylish and comfortable house, but their main wish was for a beach house that looked as if it belonged in the jungle.

The challenge for the architect was to create a new house, but to retain the prefabricated steel structure already on the site. A further difficulty was encountered in relation to the carpentry and the supply of wood for the house. The wood was eventually sourced from Para in the north of Brazil, and modified to provide the effects desired by the architect. The wood provides the element of rusticity desired by the clients, and it will continue to weather and change in appearance.

Doors and window frames were carefully designed to capture the expansive views; water and plants were thoughtfully incorporated into the design of the house.

Despite its large size (5380 square feet/500 square meters), the house is harmonious, simple and sophisticated, in keeping with its beachside location.

1 Water and plants thoughtfully incorporated into design of house
2 Front façade
3 Outdoor living enhanced by warmth of Brazilian wood

1

2

4   Expansive living area
5   Minimalist bathroom
6   Upper level balcony incorporates hot tub
7   Double-height outdoor living
Photography: Tuca Reinés

4

5

6

Itapicirica da Serra Residence

São Paulo, Brazil

CARLOS BRATKE ATELIÊ DE ARQUITETURA

A new Cartesian model was developed in the planning of this 8608-square-foot (800-square-meter) house, where two perpendicular axes provide the general circulation in the same way as two crossed streets. Spacious circuits are formed by the linkage of rooms and internal gardens, leading to the swimming pool and terraces, and to views of the large area over the nearby mountain that dominates the alpine landscape.

The 24-inch-thick (60-centimeter) walls are double and hollow, providing thermal mass and solidity to the structure. Materials used include brick, pigmented concrete, curved metal sheeting, and glass.

1

2

3

1 Gallery
2 Aerial view
3 Front view
4 Floor plan
5 View from swimming pool
6 Side view
Photography: Jose Moscardi

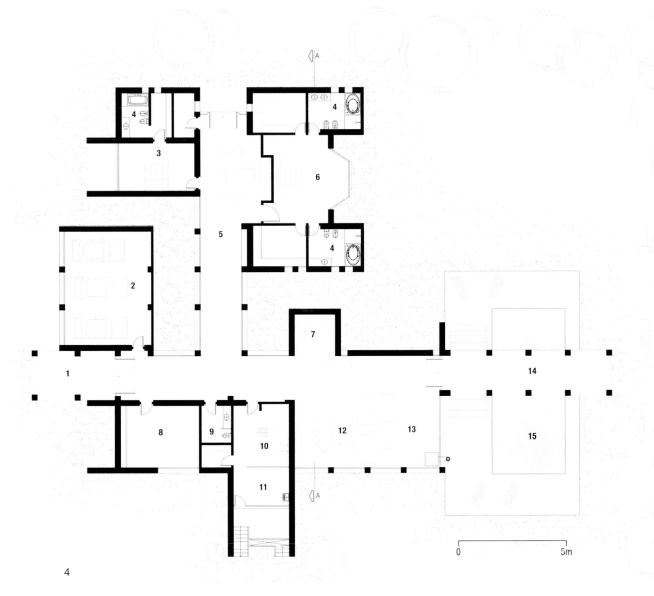

1	Entry
2	Garage
3	Bedroom
4	Bath
5	Gallery
6	Master bedroom
7	Bar
8	Office
9	Toilet
10	Kitchen
11	Laundry
12	Dining room
13	Living room
14	Terrace
15	Swimming pool

0   5m

4

5

6

Iversen Kaplan Residence

Princeton, New Jersey, USA

GARRISON ARCHITECTS

Situated in a heavily wooded area of Princeton, New Jersey, this project involved an addition to a late-modern home with vernacular influences. The existing 5000-square-foot (465-square-meter) house was turned inward, with little relationship to its natural surroundings. The project involved the design and construction of a 4000-square-foot (370-square-meter) addition that would allow nature and the existing structure to interact. Limited by the foliage of the surrounding forest, oblique sunlight was introduced through the horizontal glazing. A system of operable skylights set above a hot air reservoir works in conjunction with an internal light-diffusing layer, both to distribute light and to induce ventilation through buoyant air movement.

The residence embraces sustainability through whole building design. It incorporates building orientation, energy efficiency, sustainable material choices, and a passive ventilation system. The materials used in the house have all been subjected to a comprehensive evaluation that includes embodied energy (all of the energy required for material extraction, movement, production, and fabrication), operating energy (the energy to operate and maintain the structure), and service duration.

In this project, maple wood was specifically selected for its density and durability, which lent well to the design and final look of the home. In addition, the wood was harvested regionally and is an indigenous species to the area. The inclusion of resin panels in the design was again to provide a durable and stable light source through light-diffusing panels. Approximately 40 percent of the materials used to construct the panels were recycled and processed in an ecologically controlled manufacturing facility.

The steel windows installed have more than double the lifecycle of wood or aluminum and are low embodied energy (low-e). This particular style is made from highly recycled material, an environmentally responsible feature, important to both the architect and owner. The choice of bluestone and jet mist granite was due to the stone's density and durability, in addition to being regionally quarried and fabricated. The laminated, low-e glass provides large panes and no seal breakage, reducing the infiltration and thermal loss through metal.

1 Living room and dining room
2 View of the master bedroom cantilevered over the entry
3 View of the entry vestibule, looking out at courtyard
4 Support strut at the entrance
Photography: courtesy Garrison Architects

1

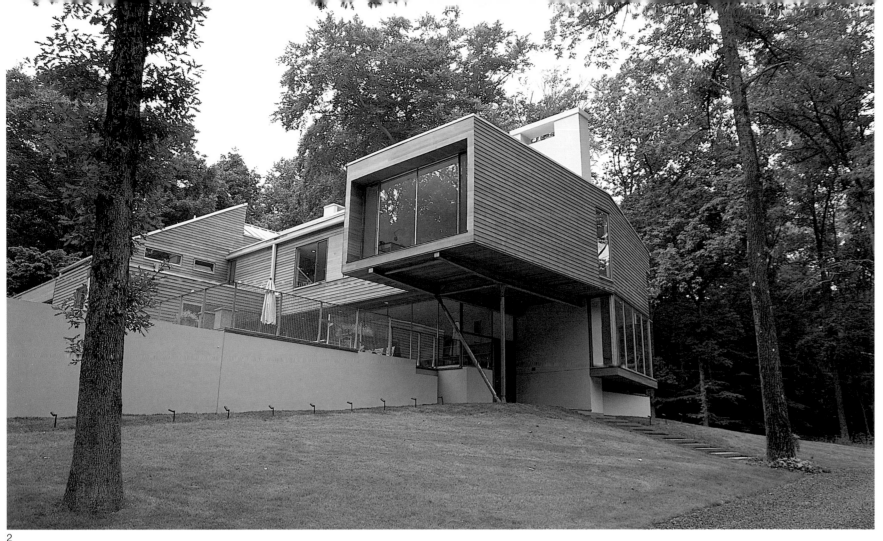

2

3

4

Kew House

Kew, Victoria, Australia

JACKSON CLEMENTS BURROWS ARCHITECTS

The Kew House is located on an existing subdivided tennis court cut into a steep site in Melbourne's inner east. The brief called for car access, and for the master bedroom and living areas to be located on the same level.

The brief provided an opportunity to design a building that immersed itself into its context, not as a stand-alone inanimate object, but as a building that contributed to and formed part of the surrounding ambiance. If the ground plane (existing tennis court) was an artificial scar on the landscape, could the new building effect a new condition that repaired, rejuvenated and reconnected with what once was? Could a built solution contribute to the ambiance of an existing location by intensifying its intangible ephemeral qualities? How do you make a building that shifts the focal point from architecture to the atmosphere it produces? These questions informed the built solution, the selection of materials, the articulation of interior volumes and the resolution of the architectural form itself.

The first-floor living platform, suspended amongst a canopy of trees and supported by a steel column system, recalls the new growth of self-seeded saplings. The two-tone cladding of the architectural form evokes the colors of the once-dominant indigenous river red gums and the satin finish of the Colorbond contrasts with the dull matt of oxidizing zinc. These are materials that accentuate the liveliness of the constant changes in the light.

The house responds to all orientations in a specific way. Every room in the house orients itself north to maximize a view corridor across the nearby golf course and the northern suburbs of Melbourne. The west and east openings are kept to a minimum, reducing heat gain and overlooking to neighboring properties and protecting the occupants from the impact of future development on both east and west boundaries.

The use of a detailed steel structure and metal building products in this project as structural and cladding elements was central to achieving the architectural intention of the project—a response that references, heals, regenerates and strengthens both the physical and atmospheric qualities of its site and surrounds.

1 Extended eaves and walls provide solar protection and privacy
2 Upper floor and living areas elevated amongst the surrounding landscape
3 Entry from the street is directly to the upper level and the unfolding view is concealed

1

2

3

4

5

6

7

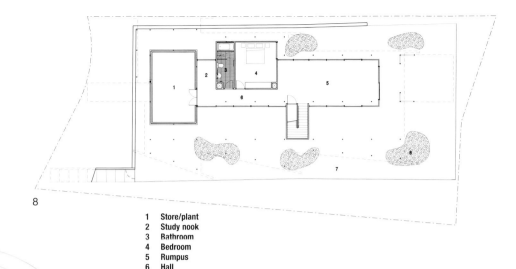

8

1 Store/plant
2 Study nook
3 Bathroom
4 Bedroom
5 Rumpus
6 Hall
7 Previous tennis court
8 Bunker

9

1 Driveway
2 Garage
3 Laundry
4 Bathroom
5 Bedroom
6 Kitchen
7 Breakfast
8 Deck
9 Entry bridge
10 Hallway
11 Front garden
12 Study/office
13 Ensuite
14 Master bedroom
15 Dining
16 Living

4 Stair access to the subterranean rumpus room from hallway
5 Living space becomes a viewing platform
6 Living spaces and kitchen are both divided and connected by the circulation spine and breezeway
7 Subterranean rumpus room opens onto remnants of tennis court
8 Upper level floor plan
9 Lower level floor plan
Photography: John Gollings, Gollings Photography Pty Ltd

King Residence

Malibu, California, USA

APPLETON & ASSOCIATES, INC. – ARCHITECTS

The site is a 7.5-acre (3-hectare) property adjacent to a State Park that was previously undeveloped and offered a remote, picturesque rural setting with California oaks, wildflower meadows, and spectacular canyon and mountain views.

The design for a new 3200-square-foot (297-square-meter) house included a separate studio/guest room/garage building and a one-bedroom main house. An entry courtyard, surrounded on three sides by walls opening out to the canyon on the fourth side, connects the two buildings. The siting on the crest of a gently sloping hill provided an opportunity to terrace the building, garden and courtyard areas to take better advantage of views to the pasture below and canyon beyond.

The main house ground floor living, dining, and kitchen areas were combined in a single, long room on the ground floor that takes advantage of the expansive canyon views to the east and opens to the west onto a covered porch and a more intimate and enclosed terraced garden with lap pool and oak trees. The 60-foot-long (18-meter) lap pool and porch colonnade reach out toward the north, extending the architecture into the landscape.

The heavy stucco walls, porches, and courtyards are based loosely on traditional southwestern precedents, but the more particular design features and details are contemporary in spirit. The corrugated metal gable and shed roofs relate to the simple barns and local ranch and farm buildings typical of this still-rustic area. The client's original ideas ranged from American Country to Luis Barragán to High Tech Contemporary. The intent was to create an architectural compound that was contemporary in spirit but colorful, warm and slightly rough around the edges.

1

2

1   Entry gate
2   Porch and colonnade and pool
3   North–south elevation
4   Front elevation
5   Archway
6   Kitchen
7   Porch and pool
Photography: Alex Vertikoff

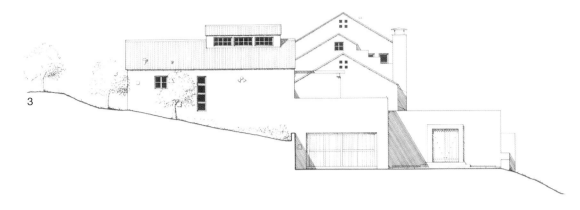

3

4

5

6

7

Kohavi House

Portola Valley, California, USA

SWATT ARCHITECTS

The Kohavi House is set in the hills overlooking Palo Alto and San Francisco Bay. Its design emphasizes the flow of space from indoors to outdoors, structural expression and connection to the land. The 4260-square-foot (396-square-meter) house is designed with an L-shaped plan which organizes the site, a 1.5-acre (0.6-hectare) east-facing knoll, into three distinct outdoor rooms: an entry court with low wood bridges on the west side, a children's play area on the north side, and a future pool and terrace on the east side.

The plan is organized around a two-story circulation spine, articulated by four cast-in-place vertical concrete frames. Doors at either end of the spine provide access to the exterior and emphasize the connection of interior and exterior spaces. Adjacent to the circulation spine, the living/dining space has been designed as a glass pavilion with a soaring, chevron-shaped, cantilevered roof that opens to panoramic views and visually extends interior space to the outdoors.

2

1   Overall view from south
2   Living/dining pavilion at night

3

6

4

5

7

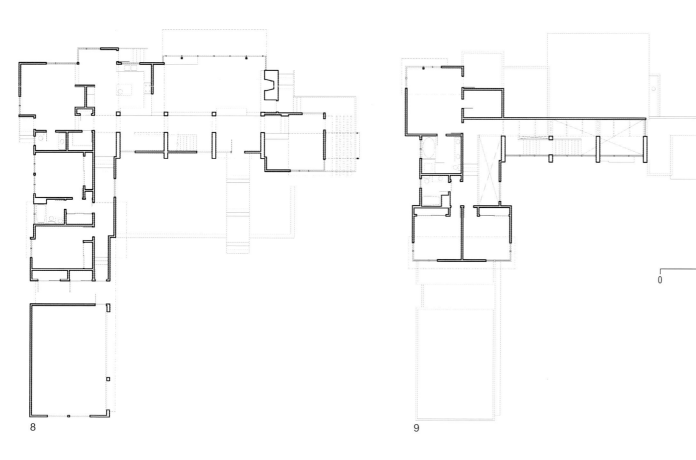

8

9

0   16ft

3 Living/dining room
4 Living room
5 View of stair from living room
6 Entrance elevation
7 Kitchen
8 Lower level floor plan
9 Upper level floor plan
Photography: Cesar Rubio, Richard Barnes

Lake Harriet Home

Minneapolis, Minnesota, USA

CHARLES R. STINSON ARCHITECTS

Aficionados of art and architecture, the clients wished to return to city life and build a new home on an urban lake. The clients sketched a simple floor plan, encompassing all of their ideas and dreams. They wanted their new Minneapolis home to be a combination of Chicago-meets-New York loft. The architects, in close collaboration with the clients, created a living space of warm wood, natural light and expansive views that complement an industrial, loft-like aesthetic of steel and glass.

The site of the 5000-square-foot (465-meter) home is organized by a circular auto court created as a bike race-track for children. A curving bluestone wall references the auto court circle while creating a private yard overlooking the lake, allowing the family to be part of the busy culture of the lake, but maintaining privacy because of the height of the windows, columns and walls. The home's horizontal and vertical forms step back on the site, allowing light to reach every room. Clerestory windows in the great room lift the space, balanced by soffits, which preserve a more intimate scale.

Architectural details throughout the house include a museum-style reveal between the walls and baseboards, and exposed plywood corners on cabinetry that celebrates the wood's striated layers.

Energy and light are the key points of the architecture; the horizontal and vertical forms of the house celebrate the movement of energy, and create a pleasurable family environment.

1 Lakeside elevation with curving bluestone wall and private lawn
2 Intersecting horizontal and vertical planes detailed at guest entrance

1

2

3 Dining room looking north toward great room and lake
4 Master bath suite overlooking lake
5 Foyer's floor-to-ceiling windows highlight seamless
   transitions between inside and outside
6 Great room with lofted ceiling is accentuated by window
   seat and intimate kitchen
7 Main suite with deck overlooking lake
Photography: Peter Bastianelli-Kerze

4

3

5

6

7

Lantern House

Cronulla, New South Wales, Australia

DEM (AUST) PTY LTD

The concept behind this 4840-square-foot (450-square-meter) waterfront home is the idea of layered translucency. Glass is the main medium—used traditionally for vision, sandblasted for screening, colored for light enhancement, strengthened for stairs and bridges, and used as a substrate for finely sliced marble sheets to create a translucent privacy façade to the public street elevation. This spider-marble and glass veneer filters sunlight in the morning to the main bedroom suite and at night glows like a Chinese onyx lantern.

The circulation spine and stairs on the northern boundary are all in glass. Additional sandblasted external glass screens and extensive external louvers allow light deep into the home, while providing privacy and climatic control. A pond, water feature and the raised pool extend the northern spine out to the nearby bay.

Bright accent colored glass is used on the western elevation: reds, yellows, and oranges complement the muted tone of the other house materials: gray steel, limestone, timber, zinc, and aluminum.

Where the house is cut into the ridge, the exposed sandstone remains, revealed as a natural backdrop. The excavated stone is reused in rough chiselled form for retaining walls and external accent—contrasting in both color and texture with the smooth and fine glass and metal in the building.

Glass-wrapped lightwells are dropped into the depth of the building to illuminate and ventilate the internal rooms. The open plan and glass internal walls allow the living spaces a series of filtered views back toward the water while allowing the owners to retreat to relative enclosure when required. The double-story family room and kitchen on the ground floor spill out onto the rear deck. The middle level contains the children's and guest bedrooms, entry, and garage. The top level is a contained parent's retreat with bedroom, bathroom, study, gym and changing room extending onto a large roof terrace.

1 Side courtyard and lap pool
2 Street elevation with marble/starfire glass panels and screens
3 Street elevation at dusk, with glowing translucent marble/starfire glass panels

1

2

4   Glass stairwell
5   Bayside elevation showing use of frameless
    glass balustrades
6   Family area opens onto decks and pool
7   Double-volume family and dining space with
    glass bridge and stairs
8   Upper level floor plan
9   Middle level floor plan
10 Ground level floor plan
11 Kitchen and double-volume family area
    opens to deck and bay beyond
Photography: Kata Bayer (1,3–5,7,11); Marian Riabic (2,6)

4

5

6

7

11

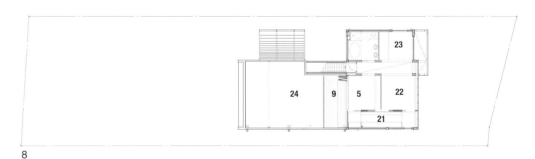

8

1	Garage	13	Games
2	Entry	14	Living
3	Lightwell	15	Lightwell/courtyard
4	Guest room	16	Veranda
5	Bedroom	17	Pool
6	Glass bridge	18	Boat shed
7	Void over family room	19	Sandstone bluff
8	Children's play area	20	Gunamatta Bay
9	Deck	21	Robe
10	Dining	22	Gym
11	Family	23	Study
12	Kitchen	24	Roof

9

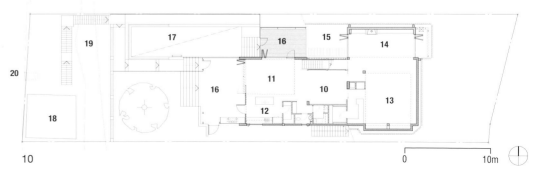

10

0   10m

Live Oak Residence

Los Feliz, California, USA

TIGHE ARCHITECTURE

The site is a wedge-shaped piece of land at the junction of two winding streets in the Hollywood Hills. The building is a continuation of the landscape, with the massing reflective of the mountainous surroundings. It is built on a substandard hillside site and subject to the hillside ordinance provisions. The project is strategically placed to not compete with the adjacent Wallace Neff house. From the parcel, a commanding view of the Griffith observatory is dominant, the omnipresent Hollywood sign is above, and the Los Angeles cityscape is in the distance.

The program consists of a painting studio, and living quarters with a loft. The spaces are processional in the sense that many experiences are had as one ascends. The interior spaces, their program and the notion of journey define the exterior form of the building. A series of framed views from which to experience the power of the site are set up along the way. Glimpses of beyond are provided in anticipation of the final destination; indirect light filters in from the stairwell shaft. The oversized sliding door opens to a direct view of the observatory. From the studio, one continues up to the loft. The stairwell is sandwiched between two walls, and storefront glazing is incorporated at each end, where the mature trees of the site are visible. The second level opens to a roof deck with a grand exterior stair. The roof terrace allows one to experience the extraordinary views. The plateau is a stage set, with the Hollywood Hills and the major icons of Los Angeles as the background.

The new building stands alone but also complements the existing by using a similar palette of materials. The building is wood frame with steel components; the exterior is stucco. The roof decks are an elastomeric membrane decking, and the grand stairs are precast concrete planks.

1   The massing is reflective of the mountainous surroundings; precast concrete planks sit atop the sloped roof plane to create a grand stair that leads to a rooftop terrace
2   View of courtyard with reflecting pool; the stair tower beyond brings light into the building

1

4

5

6

3   The office has views to the city beyond and the studio below
4   An indoor/outdoor gallery with glass walls serves as the entrance
    to the building
5   A 20-foot-tall (6-meter) sliding wall, clad in tongue and groove
    cedar, opens to the outdoors
6   View from the loft, looking down into the painting studio
Photography: Art Gray

M House

Rimini, Italy

ANTONELLO MAMBELLI ARCHITECT

This 6080-square-foot (565-square-meter) villa is located along one of the most important town planning avenues in Rimini, extending from the old town center directly to the sea front.

The four-story villa comprises a utility floor (ground floor), two floors dedicated to living space (first and second floors) and a top floor with a swimming pool and large terrace. The terrace extends to a further two-story structure housing an entertainment area with a full bar, and a fitness and wellness area.

The structure is enhanced by a rich, variegated use of innovative materials. These include the limestone covering the entrance atrium pillars as well as the façade; the inclined titanium-tinted steel shingles on the main front façade; the custom-treated aluminum of the window frames and sun break; and the satined glass of the crown balustrade of the swimming pool floor.

These elements of design, added to the complex building techniques, illustrate the synergy of precise craftsmanship and the use of modern technology. Many of the systems are automated; radiant heating is incorporated in walls and ceilings; particular attention was paid to lighting systems, and their relationship with flooring throughout the house. Much of the external flooring (entrance garden, external atrium, second-floor balcony, swimming pool terrace, and the pool itself) was designed to capture and reflect the artificial light emitted by various illumination points, including LED and optical fiber systems. These light sources are integral and active components of the project and avoid the simple and banal effects of "household lighting."

1   Detail of steel and glass bridge with
    mechanical shade in the background
2   West façade
Opposite:
    View of the main front façade showing
    steel shingles

1

2

5

6

7

4 Evening view of swimming-pool floor, overlooking fitness and wellness area
5 Entertaining area features a full bar
6 View of the living room with false ceiling
7 Bathroom features Portoro and Giallo Siena marble
Photography: Gianluca Pasquini Riccione

Maison Kawsara

Dakar, Sénégal

VICTOR LÉVY DESIGN & ARCHITECTURE

The brief for this new home was unusual. The owner, hailing from a notable Senegalese family, lives in Europe. The challenge was to create a seamless link between two radically different types of lifestyles and cultures.

Dakar, Senegal, sits squarely under the sun, wedged between the desert and the Atlantic Ocean. Respite from the elements abounds in the shade of the mango tree and in the divine ocean breeze. And it's in the flower-filled inner courtyard, where the ground is cooled by smooth, artfully laid mosaic tiles, that life gently unfolds.

The house is located in a hamlet of other villas built in the 1960s, on a lot of 3443 square feet (320 square meters). Kawsara's flower-filled inner courtyard—charmingly finished in mosaic tiles of various grays to mute the reflection of the sun—revels in the shade of two stunning trees, and is the focus of the household.

The ground floor is devoted to ordinary life functions, European style: living room, dining room, kitchen, maids' quarters and children's bedrooms. All bedrooms are self-sufficient, each equipped with its own shower and lavatory. The children's rooms connect to the living area via a hallway. Meanwhile, all rooms boast a door to the courtyard for added freedom or to welcome parents or other guests.

Access to the master suite, higher up, runs outside the building. Rain is a rare occurrence here and the stairs are comfortable enough to tackle effortlessly, in slippers. At the top of the stairs is a vast terrace, shaded by a wooden pergola, which also shelters the entire house from the sun's relentless rays. This terrace dominates the neighborhood. It is where meals are taken, atop plain, Senegalese floor mats. Alongside this terrace is the master bedroom, flanked by its own walk-in dressing room and luxurious bathroom.

The house was built using local supplies and local, skilled labor. Materials include concrete blocks for the walls, metallic fittings for all doors and windows, and tropical wood for the sun-filtering pergola. Drawing inspiration from the shade of the mango tree, the architect opted to create as much shade as possible on the walls and rooftop by casting a series of protruding, arched concrete sun caps over the house, in addition to the pergola. Ceilings were kept deliberately high to draw hot air out of the living quarters; simple but efficient cross-ventilation ensures a delightful coolness.

1 Terrace with mango tree
2 & 4 View from street
3 Staircase and wooden pergola
5 Axonometric
Photography: Fabien de Cugnac

1

2

3

4

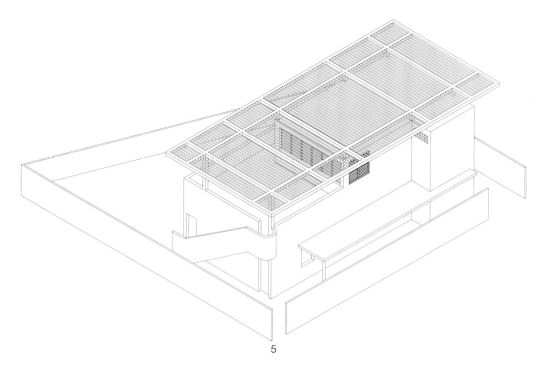

5

Malibu Meadows Residence

Calabasas, California, USA

ALEKS ISTANBULLU ARCHITECTS

The brief for this house was the addition of a master suite and screened-in porch/family room to an existing single-family, ranch-style home located on 3.5 acres (1.5 hectares) of land in rustic Malibu Canyon.

Creating a tree-house feeling, the architect raised the master suite to hover among the branches of a vast grove of California oaks. Defined by vertical redwood slats, the addition's exterior wall curves out, creating a cozy, light-filled reading nook in the master bedroom. The curved exterior wall also slopes gently upward, serving both practical and aesthetic purposes. Inside the master suite, large, operable windows and skylights infuse the room with dappled light that filters through the wood latticework. A built-in travertine fireplace adds a contemporary elegance to the room. The upstairs master bath also takes advantage of the surrounding trees, with windows and skylights strategically placed to frame views, bring in light, and ensure privacy. A central vanity island with a fossilized marble top features facing sinks, back-to-back mirrors, and generous hidden storage. The open bathtub area elegantly merges luxurious materials of limestone and maple with the feeling of outdoor bathing.

On the ground level, below the master suite, is a casual family room designed as a screened-in porch. Enclosed by mesh screen on all three sides facing the garden and oak grove, and featuring a curvilinear wood wall and a green Venetian plaster ceiling, the room has a cabin-like feeling. Creating a transitional foyer, the architects opened up the existing kitchen wall to create an open space that connects the enclosed porch and master suite with the main house. Defined by the vertical maple wood lattice of the new stairway, the foyer also houses hidden storage, and a bathroom nestled under the stairs. The curved wall separating the bathroom's tiled shower from the screened-in family room echoes the soft curves of the reading nook above.

Redwood on the exterior and a combination of cherry and maple in various finishes on the interior complement the owners' collection of traditional furniture. Venetian plaster in green on the first-floor ceiling, and blue on the second-floor ceiling evoke the surrounding trees and sky. The limestone fireplace in the bedroom and fossilized marble in the master bathroom add luxury to the addition's rustic feeling.

1 Curved reading nook follows shape of the building
2 Bathroom is replete with windows looking into the woods
3 Redwood slats cover the undulating upper volume
4 Green Venetian plaster outdoors and in maintains the woodland theme
5 Porch is screened in on three sides for maximum views, light, and air
6 Indoor/outdoor family room is used year-round for dining and gatherings
Photography: Ciro Coelho

1

2

3

4

5

6

Menteng Residence

Jakarta, Indonesia

PARAMITA ABIRAMA ISTASADHYA, PT

The brief for this corner site was a residence with large rooms, which created concerns for the provision of adequate natural lighting and ventilation. The solution was to incorporate a semi-basement to house service areas, a multifunction room and the garage. This arrangement allows the living areas to open to views of gardens and small courts that allow light and air to penetrate the dense massing. Care was taken with finishes and exotic motifs to create an atmosphere of imported luxury.

The interiors are organized around a central two-story hall, which is also the family sitting area. This high dramatic space also serves as a source of light for much of the upper circulation areas. The master bedroom is situated next to the swimming pool and has an adjoining sunroom, which is set between the garden and a small light court—it has become the favorite room in the house for afternoon tea.

1 Main entrance to foyer
2 Front elevation
3 Pool at night

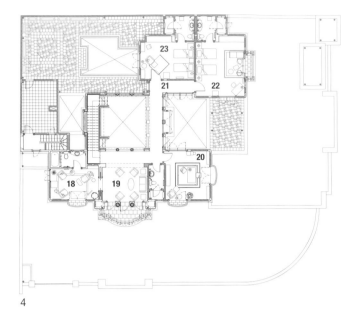

220

4

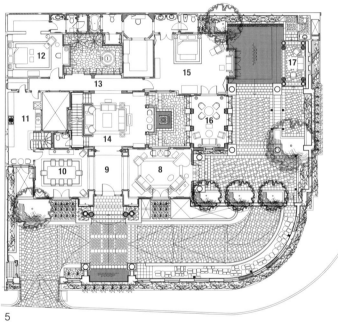

5

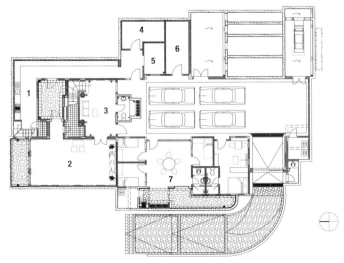

6

7

8

4   Upper level floor plan
5   Ground level floor plan
6   Basement level floor plan
7   Family room
8   Backyard
9   Pool next to master bedroom
10 Formal dining room
Photography: Okky Soetrisno

9

10

Mountain Cabin

California, USA

WALKER WARNER ARCHITECTS

The clients' love for this beautiful mountainous region began many years before they decided to build a weekend cabin there. Their wish was that the buildings would be as minimal in size as possible, respecting the land and the pace of life that unfolds there. They asked that the indoor/outdoor connections be maximized so that rooms could borrow space and beauty from the surrounding landscape. They envisioned a cabin that would slip into the landscape as if it had always been there, and always would be. This cabin would be passed down through the family from generation to generation.

The architects' goal was to make the cabin as flexible and efficient as possible. Rooms were designed to spill out into the site with 10-foot-wide (3-meter) sets of doors opening to the meadow. Communal living spaces in the cabin were created to provide more expansive spaces for nighttime activities. The bulk of the cabin was reduced by employing built-ins throughout, to give rooms ship-like efficiency, and by lowering plate heights to make rooms cozy and intimate. Doors and windows push dormers above the main roof plane where necessary and fill between members of the timber frame to give the cabin a strong sense of connection between indoors and out. As a result, no room feels crowded. Each shares the expansiveness of the immediate and distant views beyond.

The material palette and detailing were approached with three goals: to allow the site and cabin to flow into one another, to use environmentally sourced materials, and to give the cabin a sense of permanence. The material palette was reduced to essentials: wood, steel, and stone. The materials appear both on the interior and the exterior of the cabin, blurring the line between inside and out. Minimal detailing allows the full beauty of the materials to be revealed without the distraction of fussy details. A timber frame was an ideal solution to a short building season and the desire to use reclaimed material. Additionally, stone was salvaged from a ranch where a quarry had been abandoned a hundred years ago. Granite that had been split and then left to weather in the elements was carefully installed to expose its natural patina. Artisans were brought in to share their special talents. Custom elements, from light fixtures to sinks carved from blocks of stone, give the cabin the feeling of a rare gem.

1   View across pond to cabin and meadow
Opposite:
    View through dining room doors to granite peaks

1

3

1 Loft
2 Loft alcove
3 Dressing room
4 Master bath
5 Master bedroom
6 Balcony
7 Open to below

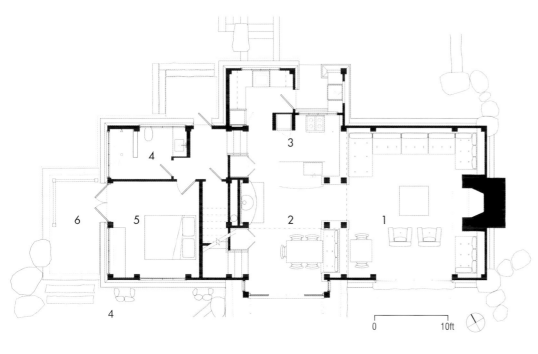

4

0   10ft

1 Living
2 Dining
3 Kitchen
4 Guest bathroom
5 Guest bedroom
6 Guest deck

3 Upper level floor plan
4 Lower level floor plan
5 Built-in bench under low eave
6 Living room fireplace
7 Bedrooms open to balcony and deck
8 Dining room bay and adjacent deck
9 Stone tub in master bath
Photography: Cesar Rubio

5

6

7

8

9

Nautilus

Rancho Mirage, California, USA

PATEL ARCHITECTURE; NARENDRA PATEL, AIA

Approaching the house, the captivating sculptural form, natural materials, soft desert colors and curving walls gently guide the visitor through the metal gates into the front courtyard. Natural stone-faced walls are set off against simple elegant stucco forms, emphasizing form and volume.

The drama is intensified as one walks through the front door. Walls begin sweeping from the outside, through the transparent glass barriers inside and back again, and out the other end to the water view. The hovering vaulted ceiling creates the illusion of a floating cover to this indoor/outdoor visual living experience. The inspiration for this house came to the architect from a seashell. The mathematical formula from the DaVinci code and the conical shape of the nautilus became the inspiration and derivation for his translation of this home's design.

The 5,900-square-foot (550-square-meter) home comprises a master bedroom with his-and-her bathrooms and closets, a living room with sunken bar, dining room, kitchen leading to family room, an office, a second bedroom, a large gym, and a complete guest house. A 1000 square-foot (93-square-meter), three-car garage completes the program.

All interior walls are covered with Venetian plaster. The natural stone wall continues from the outside, penetrating the glass wall barrier as it flows through the living room. The roof is copper and the floors limestone. The ceiling is tongue-and-groove wood, punctured with myriad small halogen lights producing the effect of a star-studded sky.

The floating ceiling effect is achieved by steel columns and beams combined with open web steel bar trusses and wood framing. This is accentuated by exterior walls, which are separated from this large vault by clerestory windows and the intermediary dividing walls, freestanding and much lower than the curved ceiling itself. An illusion of space and volume, with the outdoor sky visible from all directions, creates the effect of a seemingly free-standing roof.

This home was designed using the principles of sustainable design, resulting in a building that is environmentally responsible and a healthy place to live. This was achieved by implementing energy efficient lighting, heat and cooling; specifying environmentally friendly green building and construction methods; orienting the glazed area and living spaces to achieve low energy usage; installation of plumbing fixtures with reduced water usage; and the introduction of native arid landscaping, to achieve water savings.

1

2

1 Sculptural entry courtyard
2 View of family room and breakfast room open to kitchen
3 Interior opens to outdoors with floating roof

4

6

5

7

8

9

4 Nautilus-inspired great room
5 Powder room
6 Master suite with custom-designed bed wall
7 Living room with hovering ceiling
8 Outdoor living room with seemingly suspended roof
9 Dining room looks out to courtyard; dining table
   with Chihully vase, entry foyer in background
Photography: Arthur Coleman

Nelson Residence

Philo, California, USA

HOUSE + HOUSE ARCHITECTS

Located two hours north of San Francisco in the California wine country, this home with an interior garden courtyard and deep-set porches manifests a serene form in an untamed landscape. Designed for an industrial designer and an artist, the retreat is completely wrapped with corrugated galvanized steel, reflecting the sky and trees, changing color throughout the day, sometimes sparkling, sometimes invisible.

The 25-acre (10-hectare) site in the Anderson Valley, part of a former horse ranch, consisted of mature oaks, pines and Douglas fir trees on rolling hills covered with wild California grasses. The program called for interconnected kitchen, dining and living spaces, a master suite, a guest room/library with bath, an art studio, utility area and garage. A knoll on the property with a southwestern exposure and spectacular views was selected for the house site.

The guiding force behind the house's form included the desire for open space, connection to the outdoors and access to natural sunlight. By wrapping the home around an interior courtyard, each room enjoys natural light from two opposite sides. Deep-set porches on the south and west offer shade from the harsh summer sun and provide covered outdoor space. Broad expanses of composed windows puncture the walls to frame carefully selected views to the canyons and hills beyond as well as into the central garden courtyard where a Japanese maple tree and rock fountain provide a tranquil meditation area within the home.

Simplicity and functionality were considered in the finish materials. An 8-foot-square (2.5-meter) glass entry door set in a red steel frame is a strong geometric element as one approaches the house. Corrugated galvanized steel siding and roofing are anchored with a red concrete column supporting the roof overhang. In the home's interior, black slate floors, bleached maple cabinetry with zinc and stone counters and industrial light fixtures complete a simple palette and provide a clean modern backdrop for the owners' eclectic collection of paintings, furniture, ceramics and ethnic art.

1 Exterior view from west
2 Entry door detail
3 Dining room with view to courtyard
4 Entry vestibule
5 Master bedroom
6 Master bath vanity with view to bedroom
Photography: Steven House

1

2

3

4

5

6

New York Town House

New York, New York, USA

ALEXANDER GORLIN ARCHITECTS

Set back 25 feet (7.6 meters) from the street, this black glass jewel of a town house has become a landmark that defines the neighborhood around it. Originally built in 1958, the shabby two-story structure had fallen into disrepair, and was completely redesigned, extended vertically, and in part restored. Mid-century modern was brought into the 21st century.

The new glass façade of the house announces its presence on the street, and a red door marks the entry once hidden inside the low brick wall defining the private precinct of the house. Inside, an open loft space of living, dining, and kitchen are open to the exterior with large glass walls on either side. A new staircase with open treads leads to the upper levels, within an atrium filled with light from the expansive skylight above. The second level has two children's bedrooms with a master bedroom on the street side. The master bath, with walls and floors of white statuary slab marble and glass, is open to the bedroom with a long line of elegant pear wood closets leading from one space to the other. The addition of the third level is marked by glass block floors that allow light to penetrate deep into the floors below.

The culmination of the house is the media room, which is acoustically isolated and open on one side to a terrace and on the other to the atrium with extremely clear low iron content glass. The room is framed by pear wood cabinets, which hold the owner's extensive collection of CDs within a double-layered system of shelves and doors. Also on this upper level are a guest room and an office. On the half-level below the street is the playfully colored children's playroom and exercise area. A Zen-inspired stone and moss garden provides a contemplative vestibule or air lock to allow a transition from the hectic city street to the peaceful home within.

1 Kitchen with translucent LUMAsite cabinetry filters natural light
2 Glowing glass jewel façade set back from 85th Street

1

3

3 Living room from dining table
4 View from master bath to bedroom vestibule
5 Section facing west
6 Second floor landing illuminated by skylight and glass block flooring
7 Living room from entry stair
8 Master bedroom
9 Third floor media room with steamed beech cabinets and view to landing
Photography: Peter Aaron/Esto

4

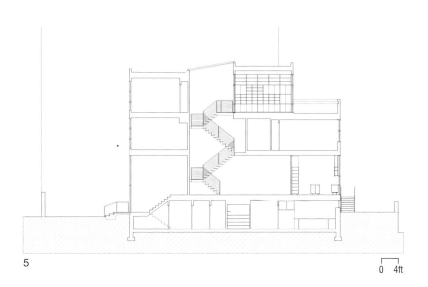

5

0 4ft

6

7

8

9

Newton House

Castlecrag, New South Wales, Australia

STANIC HARDING PTY LTD

The Newton House is the result of major alterations to an existing 1960's house for a couple making the move from a suburban terrace house to the bush suburb of Castlecrag. They now find themselves in a carefully sited multilevel house with considered connections to water views, bushland and surrounding treetops.

Early in the design stage it was obvious that the existing house would need to be almost completely rebuilt. This was due to its poor orientation on the steep sloping site, its lack of connection to the landscape plus poor existing light infiltration and limited ventilation opportunities. The 2475-square-foot (230-square-meter) renovated house now consists of three levels, the upper level being made up of the garage/driveway and roof terrace. The middle level comprises the entry courtyard, living/dining and kitchen spaces, as well as the master bedroom. A second bathroom and further bedrooms make up the lower level.

The entry courtyard links the kitchen and interior living areas to northern light, and forms an exterior room. A large deck is the connection between the interior and the surrounding bushland and treetops beyond. The roof deck adjoining the garage/driveway continues this link, allowing views out to Middle Harbour.

A 13-foot-high (4-meter) laminated glass wall acts as a suntrap, compensating for the existing orientation, flooding the living space with natural light. The resultant effect is the enlivening of a simple robust white interior complemented by the sensitive use of timber, colored glass, stainless steel and stone.

Leading down to the two bedrooms and the second bathroom is a stair with its point of origin in the living room, ultimately culminating in the open landscape of the garden area, which is a combination of natural bushland and a hovering timber platform.

1

2

3

4

1 Lower living space windows fold away
   with timber sill as seat
2 Simple composition offers strong
   expression to rear façade
3 Lower level bathroom allows private
   outdoor connection when bathing
4 Entry level spaces open onto north-
   facing courtyard

5

6

7

8

9

5 Stairwell element openings arranged to frame specific views
6 Winter sun penetrates north-facing living space that connects to trees
7 Joinery unit screens raised kitchen from living/dining space
8 Colored glass vanity shelf floats over timber storage seats
9 Detail view from garden showing framed terrace adjacent to living space
10 Lower level floor plan
11 Upper level floor plan
Photography: Paul Gosney

1 Entry courtyard
2 Living area
3 Dining area
4 Living deck
5 Kitchen
6 Storeroom
7 Study
8 Bathroom/ensuite
9 Robe
10 Master bedroom
11 Stair link
12 Lower bathroom
13 Laundry
14 External store
15 Store
16 Study/bedroom
17 Bedroom
18 Garden deck
19 Garden terrace
20 Bush garden

No. 4

Andalucia, Spain

THOMAS DE CRUZ ARCHITECTS/DESIGNERS; ROACH & PARTNERS DEVELOPERS

Designed by London-based architect Peter Thomas de Cruz, this spectacular contemporary house occupies a hillside site inland from the coast of southern Spain. The brainchild of the developers, the house challenges the orthodoxy of much of the recent pseudo-vernacular development in the area with calm, flowing spaces, a considered response to topography and climate and simplicity in detail.

With stunning views across a valley toward distant mountains in the west, this largely single-aspect house uses the slope of the site to maximum advantage. The core of the house is a top-lit, double-height gallery flooded with natural light that runs across the slope of the site. The prime living spaces are on the west side of the gallery while to the east, ancillary accommodation and cooling courtyards are set into the hillside. All of the full-height glazed façades parallel with the slope open fully to allow air to pass through the building, making the most of anabatic and katabatic winds. The cross ventilation, combined with large cantilevered roof overhangs and balconies which provide solar shading, reduces the reliance on air conditioning and extends the opportunity for comfortable open air living.

From the entrance, an elliptical curved wall on the west side peels away from the main axis, widening the gallery and pulling you toward a double-height window at the end, progressively revealing a single mountain peak in the distance. Punched holes in the gallery wall give glimpses of mountain views to the west across the series of interconnected open plan living spaces. The end of the gallery culminates in a large double-height living space that leads toward a disappearing edge swimming pool which projects out into space. At first-floor level, a bridge open on both sides overlooking the main living space leads to the master bedroom suite, which is connected to a private study below by a spiral staircase wrapped within the "tail" of the curved wall.

Adding to the sense of spectacle, the house is dramatically cut in two, with a glass-floored dining space bridging the gap between the two halves and linking the cooking space to the living space. The parallel gallery sits astride an internal pool and, when all the glazing is fully retracted, both the gallery and the dining space become bridges fully open to the air. The calmness of the house is accentuated by water flowing from the gallery courtyard pool down over a slate-finished waterfall beneath the dining room to meet the lowest of the two connected swimming pools.

1 View over the pool from the living space, looking west
2 Sliding glass doors disappear into the walls to open up the double-height gallery to external space and pools on both sides
Opposite:
   Main entrance showing cantilevered canopy with double-height gallery behind

1

2

4 First floor plan
5 Ground floor plan
6 Kitchen terrace looking toward the two pools
7 West-facing elevation showing deep overhanging eaves
8 Double-height living space
9 Dining space on the glass "bridge" over water running between two pools
10 Kitchen
Photography: Simon Collins

242

4

1 Living space
2 Library
3 Dining space
4 Kitchen
5 Gallery
6 Downstairs bedroom
7 Utility room
8 Internet room
9 Bathroom
10 Pantry
11 Study
12 Guest bedroom
13 Swimming pool
14 Pool
15 Bedroom
16 Void

5

6

7

8

9

10

Northwest Family Retreat

Washington, USA

OLSON SUNDBERG KUNDIG ALLEN ARCHITECTS

1 The interior of the main living space flows seamlessly to the garden and trout stream beyond

3 Concrete floors, plaster walls, steel beams, and wood ceiling combine to express an open, lodge-like feel in the main living space

2 Natural landscaped entry with stair tower, sunscreen and trellis

4 Open master bath with curved walls of plaster and glass mosaic

Designed for an active family, this residence is centered on a common area that supports a wide range of activities, from cooking and dining, homework and music, to curling up with a book by the fire. At the same time, the space makes a visually seamless connection to a natural outdoor garden area.

Set among great trees, the often filtered light enters the house and plays off the interior spaces in myriad ways, depending on the time of day and the season. The integrity of the home's materials was also an important factor in the design—solid woods, concrete, and copper were selected because they stand up to family use yet improve with age. Niches and wall surfaces are carefully placed for the display of art and objects, so that these elements are integrated into the architectural fabric. A sophisticated home theater and complete automation system are also included.

1

2

3

4

5   Upper level plan
6   Main level plan
7   Natural materials and integrated mural by Mary Ann
    Peters blend to form harmonious whole
8   Vaulted wine cellar constructed from board-formed
    concrete
9   View from main living space to dining and kitchen area,
    stairs and entry to right
10 Stairs are built of steel, with massive oak treads recycled
    from an old whiskey warehouse
Photography: Eduardo Calderon

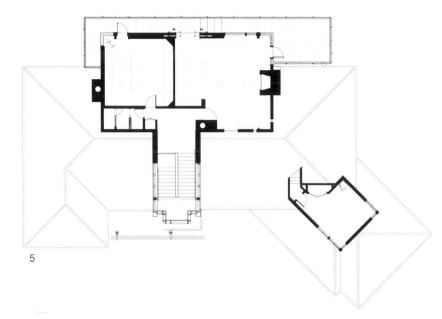

5

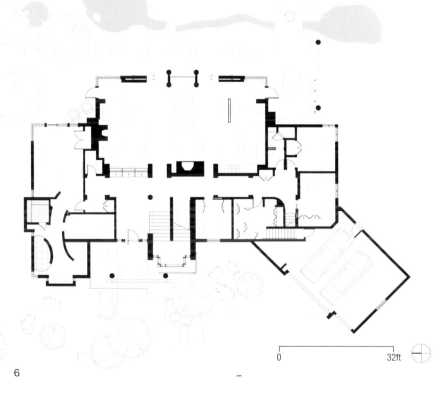

6

0   32ft

7

8

9

10

The Old Dairy

London, UK

THOMAS DE CRUZ ARCHITECTS/DESIGNERS

When the owners bought this former dairy, set amongst the 19th-century residential terraces of south London, it had already been converted into a house. However the rear courtyard and collection of outbuildings remained ramshackle and undeveloped. The owners, who had considered moving to Sydney, were inspired by houses overlooking Sydney Harbour and chose to work with London-based architect Peter Thomas de Cruz whose practice draws on subtropical design influences to breathe light and life into the stuffy English housing stock.

The traditional Victorian frontage belies the fact that the house has been completely remodeled in a contemporary manner. The existing staircase filled the hallway, cutting the house in two. By removing the staircase and locating a new one to one side of the hallway, the architects were able to free up space and create a new vista from the front door right through to the end of the rear courtyard garden. Bright light, even on the grayest London days, now draws you through the hallway and into a spacious living/dining/kitchen space that spans the full width of the house. To create the living space, a large extension has been inserted between the side access from the street and an original two-story rear addition. By removing all visible means of supporting the existing addition and the original rear wall of the house, the rear ground floor of the existing house has been seamlessly connected to the new extension to form one coherent space.

Drawing on a response to subtropical climate for inspiration, the house has been opened up to the rear courtyard across almost its whole width, with folding/sliding doors, an overhanging canopy roof and a level floor finish that blurs the division between inside and outside. The zinc-finished extension roof is pitched upward, away from the building to draw light and views of the surroundings and sky into the living space. Using tall glazing and rooflights, the previously dark, cellular layout has been liberated by an outward-looking aspect and an abundance of natural light.

The outward-looking theme of the ground floor has been carried through to the second-floor level, where a large loft space has been converted and extended to create a master bedroom suite with the feeling of a penthouse apartment. Making the most of the low-scale nature of the city, folding/sliding doors, a frameless glass balustrade and rooflights generate a sense of space by providing views over the neighboring rooftops.

1   Entrance hall
2   Study
3   Reception
4   Kitchen
5   Living/dining room
6   Studio/office
7   Garden
8   Family room

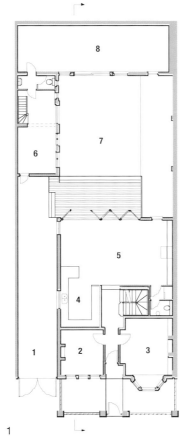

1

3

2

1   Ground floor plan
2   View of the Victorian front elevation
3   Rear view from courtyard garden
4   Courtyard garden looking toward old dairy outbuildings
5   Detail of new stair, showing frameless glass wall
6   Living space showing roof light at junction of old and the new
7   Master bedroom showing frameless glass balustrade
Photography: Andy Carver (4,7)

4

5

6

7

Old Mission Cottage

Grand Traverse Bay, Michigan, USA

BOHLIN CYWINSKI JACKSON

Located along the western shore of Old Mission Peninsula in Lake Michigan's Traverse Bay, this modest house is a reinterpretation of the aged cabins the owners are fond of visiting during their summer vacations. It also reflects a simpler and more relaxed life of long, warm, summer days, of quiet, cool evenings with a fire, of sailing, reading, and baking fruit pies. In activity and in structure, the 2400-square-foot (223-square-meter) house revolves around the centrally positioned fireplaces and wood-burning stove. This chimney mass, constructed of concrete planks and left unfinished to reveal the grain of wood forms, is the heart of the house.

Winding through the forest, one approaches the house from the east, revealing the cottage's flesh-colored "face." Windows form the eyes and mouth while an exhaust vent is the nose. A round column of slender wood posts resting on a large boulder marks the entry. This precise column finds its counterpoint in a massive gnarled maple trunk near the house's heart.

In material and detail, the house is both a modest cottage and a rigorous structure. Memories of other cottages abound: a quintessential stair lit by high south sun and a porch of splayed columns facing west through the forest toward the lake at dusk. Exposed Douglas fir framing and paneling, galvanized steel roofing, and unfinished concrete retain their basic nature.

Designed and constructed over ten years, this house is a testament to the patient collaboration of owner, architect, and builder.

1 View to south from entry
2 View from southwest corner
3 West elevation

1

2

5

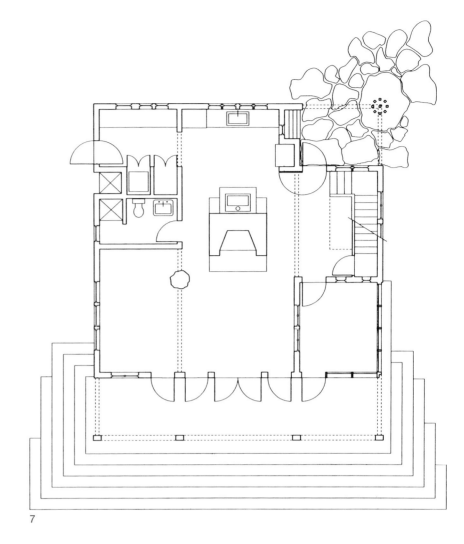

7

4   View of maple tree from living room
5   Fireplace in master bedroom
6   View of living room from dining room
7   First floor plan
Photography: Dan Bibb (1–3); Karl Backus (4–6)

6

Orange Grove

West Hollywood, California, USA

PUGH + SCARPA

Located in a neighborhood characterized by traditional bungalow-style single-family residences, Orange Grove is a new landmark for the City of West Hollywood. The building is sensitively designed and compatible with the neighborhood, but differs in material palette and scale from its neighbors. Referencing architectural conventions of modernism rather than the pitched roof forms of traditional domesticity, the project is consistent with the eclectic and often unconventional demographic of West Hollywood. Distinct from neighboring structures, the building creates a strong relationship to the street by virtue of its large amount of highly usable balcony area in the front façade.

While there are dramatic and larger scale elements that define the building, it is also broken down into comprehensible human-scale parts. Orange Grove displays a similar kind of iconoclasm as the Schindler House, an icon of California modernism, located a short distance away. Like the Schindler House, the conventional architectural elements of windows and porches become part of an abstract sculptural ensemble. At the Schindler House, windows are found in the gaps between structural concrete wall panels. At Orange Grove, windows are inserted in gaps between different sections of the building.

The design of Orange Grove is generated by a subtle balance of tensions. Building volumes and the placement of windows, doors and balconies constitute an active three-dimensional composition in motion. Each piece of the building is a strong and clearly defined shape, such as the use of two square-profile balcony surrounds in the front façade—one is small, the other large; one is open at the front, the other is veiled with stainless steel slats. At the same time each balcony is balanced and related to other elements in the building, the smaller one to the driveway gate below and the other to the roll-up door and first floor balcony. Each building element is intended to read as an abstract form in itself—such as a window becoming a slit or windows becoming a framed box, while also becoming part of a larger whole. Although this building may not mirror the status quo, it answers to the desires of consumers in a burgeoning niche market who want large, simple interior volumes of space, and a paradigm based on space, light and industrial materials of the loft rather than the bungalow.

1 View along Orange Grove Avenue
2 Rear of building from Fairfax Avenue
3 South elevation of the buildings
4 Primary living space of Unit 5
5 Unit 1 main entry on street
6 Principal living space of Unit 1
Photography: Marvin Rand

1

2

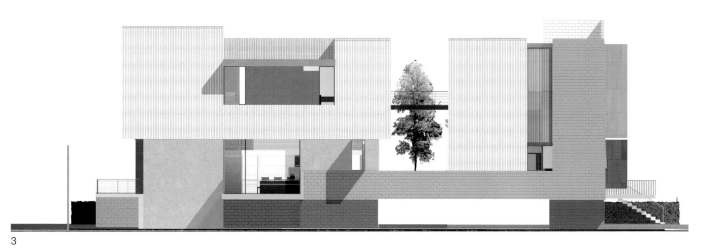

3

4

5

6

Orleans House

Cape Cod, Massachusetts, USA

CHARLES ROSE ARCHITECTS INC

The 6-acre (2.5-hectare) site is located on a bluff overlooking Pleasant Bay, Nauset Beach, and the Atlantic Ocean. The house, which traces and reinforces a naturally occurring bowl in the landscape, is sited on a slight ridge gaining water views and protecting the inland landscape. The L-shaped organization of the house creates an intimate entry landscape and orients a series of rooms to the water and southern light.

The southern wing of the 6000-square-foot (557-square-meter) house is a spacious single-level volume: the foyer, gallery, living room, dining room, and kitchen open onto each other but remain distinct with stepped floor levels and deliberately positioned walls for art. The south and west edges of the main house spill into the landscape as a series of stepped exterior terraces. Roof overhangs and sunscreen trellises shelter and shade interior and exterior spaces. At the knuckle of the L is the vertical spine of the house, an open stair providing light and access to the wine cellar, the guest bedroom levels, and an upper sitting room nested beneath a roof monitor.

To the west of the main house is a tower structure with a second floor office: this room captures sweeping views to the north, east, and south. The family room is linked to the house by a covered walk which also serves to shield the parking area from the entry landscape. A guesthouse is sited on a knoll to the north. A painting studio on the ground floor has large rolling barn doors opening to the south and the view.

1

2

1 South façade looking west
2 Tower with office on second floor
3 View into dining room

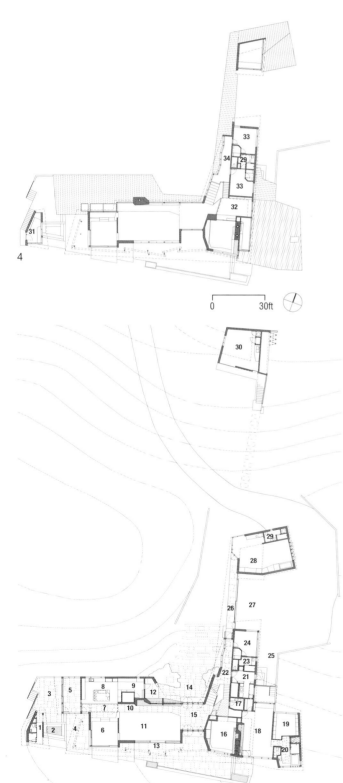

0   30ft

4

5

6

1	Cabana	20	Master bathroom
2	Spa	21	Laundry
3	West terrace	22	Lower hallway
4	Dining terrace	23	Bathroom
5	Screen porch	24	Bedroom
6	Dining room	25	Laundry entry
7	Sitting area	26	Breezeway
8	Kitchen	27	Motor court
9	Pantry	28	Family/bunk room
10	Gallery	29	Bathroom
11	Living room	30	Studio
12	Pantry entry	31	Office
13	South terraces	32	Sitting room/mezzanine
14	North entry	33	Bedroom
15	Foyer	34	Upper hallway
16	Library/media room	35	Guest bedroom
17	Powder room	36	Kitchenette
18	Master bedroom	37	Terrace
19	Master wardrobe		

4 Upper level and tower floor plan
5 Lower level floor plan
6 Living room
7 Stair
8 Family room
Photography: John Edward Linden

7

8

Oshry Residence

Bel Air, California, USA

ZOLTAN E. PALI, FAIA; STUDIO PALI FEKETE ARCHITECTS (SPF:a)

The site for the Oshry Residence was the inspiration for the project's design, requiring creative solutions to complex environmental factors. Strict zoning guidelines for hillside lots, poor soil conditions, dynamic programmatic requirements, desired adjacencies, and wide panoramic views posed critical challenges to the building's occupation of the site, but both client and architect envisioned the remarkable possibilities that the site offered, if the challenges could be overcome. The combined interaction of these forces resulted in a linear building configuration of two enfilade blocks connected by a bridge across a minimally landscaped courtyard. Given the size of the program (5000 square feet/465 square meters), the program offered an opportunity to integrate the outdoors into the building through a series of interior/exterior spatial penetrations. In addition, the longitudinal orientation of the house vis-à-vis the site created a highly charged east elevation, and numerous vantage points from within the house across the dramatic landscape below.

The Oshry Residence façade is straightforwardly articulated, boldly featuring the clean volumetric and programmatic elements of the structure. It is from the internal strip of space, parallel to the east façade, that one orients oneself physically within the house and visually to the surroundings. Elements such as the circulation bridge, stone screen wall, and retracting wood panels are derived from this organization. The end result is a scheme that resolves the inherent complexities of the site with the desired living conditions of the client, and furthers existing notions of materiality and transparency with seamless integration.

The house integrates major design elements with passive shading and ventilation functions, for maximum energy efficiency. Stone louvers on the first floor shade the living room without obstructing views. The glass bridge on the second floor uses operable windows that can be opened during hotter days, letting the warmer air escape from the second-story space, quickly cooling the rooms below.

1

2

1 Bridge and courtyard
2 East façade at night
3 Northeast corner at family room

4

5   6

4 North façade at family room
5 Stairway and louvers
6 View of living room from courtyard
7 Fireplace in living room
8 Second story floor plan
9 First story floor plan
Photography: John Linden

7

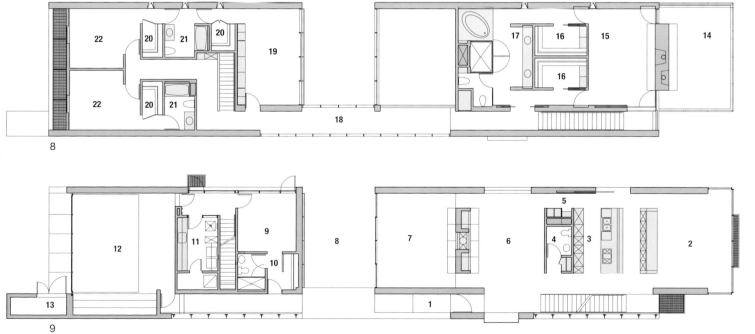

8

9

1	Entry
2	Family
3	Kitchen
4	Powder room
5	Pantry
6	Dining
7	Living
8	Courtyard
9	Maid's room
10	Bathroom
11	Utility
12	Garage
13	Storage
14	Deck
15	Master bedroom
16	Closet
17	Master bathroom
18	Bridge
19	Study
20	Closet
21	Bathroom
22	Bedroom

Overmyer Residence

Kentfield, California, USA

HOUSE + HOUSE ARCHITECTS

Perched on a southern slope in Marin County with spectacular views to Mount Tamalpias, this new 4000-square-foot (372-square-meter) home gently embraces its site. Situated on a natural shelf in a steep hillside, the home comprises two intersecting wings anchored by a tower with a butterfly roof that carefully frames the mountain peak. To take advantage of the site's limited flat area, the home is pushed to the edge of the slope to wrap around a level garden/courtyard with the upper slope gently spilling into it on one side.

The living, dining, kitchen, study and powder room have wide expanses of glass to the mountain views, spilling onto decks with invisible glass railings. High vaulted ceilings with rhythmic wood beams give definition to the large open-plan living spaces, which flow together. Clerestory windows in the north capture indirect light and large glass doors provide access to the courtyard. The tower functions as the vestibule to the private wing of the house where the master suite, two children's bedrooms and bath, and utility rooms are perpendicular to the public wing. The morning sun shines directly into the children's rooms while illuminating contained views to the mountains beyond. The courtyard is the primary outdoor space for relaxation, play and entertaining.

A meandering flagstone walkway leads from the guest parking area through a landscaped entry garden to the front door with a glass and steel canopy. Tightly spaced cedar siding and integrally colored stucco form distinctive elements that layer against one another in contrasting textures and colors. A red stucco column in the entry frames passage into the vaulted living spaces. Golden hues of stucco are sculpted into a masonry fireplace, which divides the living room from the kitchen and contains niches and cabinets for stereo equipment and art objects.

The kitchen and adjacent wet bar and seating area are bathed in natural light throughout the day. Cherry cabinetry, granite counters, hand-blown glass pendant lights and stainless steel appliances provide an elegant palette of materials. Floating vanities in the master bath in beech and cherry wood complement the subdued tones of the soft limestone flooring. All the materials are strong in nature and rich in color, creating a home that is bold, yet comfortable in its natural setting and comforting in its function as a receptacle of life.

1 View of entry courtyard from east
2 Fountain detail
Opposite:
    Exterior courtyard from northeast

1

2

1	Garage	9	Spa
2	Powder room	10	Bedroom
3	Study	11	Bedroom
4	Entry hall	12	Utility
5	Nook	13	Dressing room
6	Kitchen	14	Master bedroom
7	Dining	15	Living
8	Fountain		

4   Floor plan
5   Kitchen
6   Living area with view to courtyard
7   Fireplace detail
8   Exterior view from west
Photography: David Duncan Livingston

8

7

Palm Beach Residence

Palm Beach, Florida, USA

MOJO STUMER ASSOCIATES

This modern home of 8000 square feet (743 square meters) is located in an affluent community on a waterfront site. While there were no unusual programmatic requirements, the client wished to achieve a sense of drama in the architecture, and to capture panoramic views.

The house cmerged as two slender volumes that orient themselves perpendicular to the primary viewing plane. A double-height space connects these parallel wings. This connecting volume acts as the entry into the formal living room and dining room with full-height glass to front and back.

The circulation resulted in a progression of views: entry to the site offers a view through the center of the house. This transparency provides welcoming glimpses through to the water and sky beyond. Once inside, a 20-foot-high (6-meter) wall of glass permits a clear perception of the two wings slipping out toward the water, framing the primary view. The translucency and flow through this connecting space defines two distinctly separate wings of the house. Their imposing presence is evident throughout.

A poured concrete structural system with cinder block infill provided a stable base for an exterior stucco finish. From a massing point of view, the house is seen as a manipulation of pristine white planes and volumes that are layered in an effort to blur the true confines of the house and create a larger sense of dwelling. The interior material selection sought to maintain a cool, light-toned and low-contrast extension of the exterior walls. These vertical surfaces were seen as natural light refractors, filling the house with a soft ambient light. Materials, such as the sandy hued limestone of the central fireplace element and the light metallic grays of the window system combine with the bright white walls to present a uniform balance of cool and warm tones. Dark Brazilian mahogany was selected for the floor planes, conveying solidity and strength, and providing a sharp color contrast to the walls and a visually permanent anchor to the site.

1 Front entry door
2 Overall front entry elevation from street
3 Rear elevation seen from the water at night
4 Dining room features custom-made table by Mojo Stumer, and chiseled precast limestone fireplace wall
5 Living room looking toward floating metal staircase
Photography: Scott Francis

1

2

3

4

5

Pixel House

Heiri, South Korea

SLADE ARCHITECTURE AND MASS STUDIES

This house is for a family with two children. They are interested in the larger community and plan on sharing their exterior spaces. They intend to create a day-care center for neighboring children. The site is perfectly matched with the client's intentions—it is the last in a row of houses, at the point at which the continuous façade of the row ends. The public and private territories are not as clear as on other sites in the row.

While the public and private territories are ambiguous, the end condition is where the relationship between the building and the landscape is clearest. The entire row of houses can be read as an object/field relationship between building and landscape. The architects chose to break the row into fragments rather than just extend the row "wall" to the end of the site. Placing the main house at the western end of the site allows passage between the front and back yards and creates an outdoor space open to the street within the depth of the row house. Separating the main house volume allowed the architects to play with the relationship between landscape and building. The main volume is difficult to categorize: soft and rounded, it is somewhere between the rigid orthogonal geometry of the row and the smooth contours of the landscape.

Is it a rock or a building?

At a micro scale, this tension between the contoured natural condition and the orthogonal master plan condition is further developed in the choice of materials. By using simple orthogonal bricks, the smooth shape is digitized into discrete units. This tectonic tension between the larger smooth form and the individual bricks parallels the tension between the individual house and the row, and between the buildings and the hilly landscape.

The bricks also provide a tangible sense of scale and of the process of turning the abstract into the real. In the same way that the number of pixels determines the "smoothness" of a digital image, the smoothness of this house is determined by the size and shape of the brick.

1 Detail of large picture window and study/library inside
2 Desk at second-floor balcony and stair
3 Study/library area and stair
4 Exterior at front entry
5 View from street corner
6 Second floor plan
7 First floor plan
Photography: Yong-Kwan Kim

3

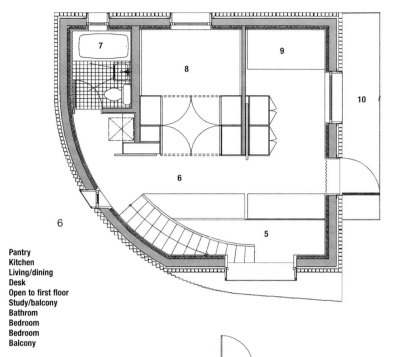

6

1 Pantry
2 Kitchen
3 Living/dining
4 Desk
5 Open to first floor
6 Study/balcony
7 Bathrom
8 Bedroom
9 Bedroom
10 Balcony

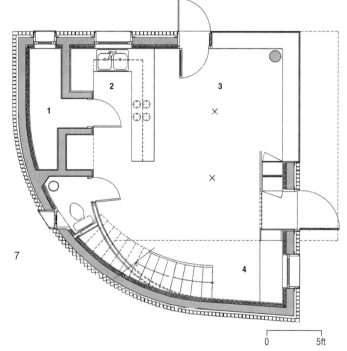

7

0   5ft

4

5

Portsea Beach House

Portsea, Victoria, Australia

BBP ARCHITECTS

Set amongst hauntingly beautiful moonah trees, this luxurious resort-style beach house provides a cul-de-sac that emerges with dramatic moments.

The home has two extensive living areas, four bedrooms, a study, and numerous bathrooms including a luxurious ensuite opening to a private courtyard space with a private spa. Because of its size, the house was designed as two interlocking wings: one for the guests and children, the other including kitchen, dining and living, the main bedroom and parents' retreat and/or second living area. The brief also included a garage area to park three cars and a boat.

To minimize the 5380-square-foot (500-square-meter) footprint of the house, the basement garage level was wedged into the site, providing a solid base to support the northeast wing. This wing acts as a rectilinear capsule with a series of cubes infiltrating its clean exterior. The cube cut-outs articulate the views, balconies and entrances. The rock wall provides a warm fabric to flank the secondary wedge, which then peels away to present the cantilevered wing. The clean parapet walls of the wedge hide a soaring light roof structure, lightly supported by a curtain of glass.

Horizontal spaces open panoramic views to the outside. To the rear of the building, the horizontality is heightened and further accentuated by the timber canopies and screens, and is only broken by the cut-outs inviting the user to weave amongst the built form and the landscape.

The deck area incorporates a large swimming pool, with an adjacent space that can either become part of the main deck area or be closed off by a pair of Japanese-style screens to become a private outdoor space to the master bedroom. The use of water is integral to the design of this house. Not only is it present in the location of the swimming pool, but also in the courtyard that intersects the two main wings of the house. An ornamental pond with continually moving water creates a contemplative feature to the living areas.

While the forms of the house are clearly modernist, the clean lines of the building have been softened by the selection of materials and colors. The house is primarily clad in timber and stone, selected to engage with the context and colors of the site.

1 Local stone wall leads to entrance
2 View from rear of property
Opposite:
    Expanse of merbau timber decking

1

2

3

4

3 Splaying roof with timber lining to underside
4 Timber sliding panels to private spa area
5 Ground floor plan
6 Basement floor plan
7 View of shower in master bedroom ensuite
8 Master bedroom with feature circular window
9 Formal living area
Photography: Shania Shegedyn

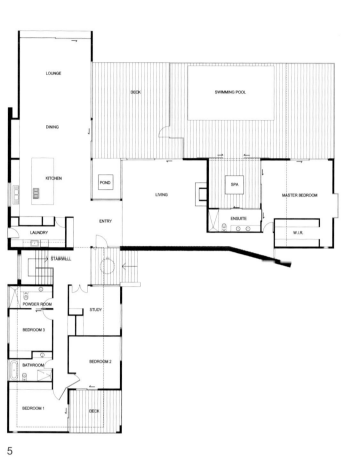

5

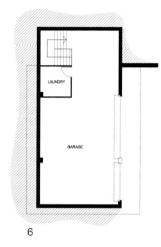

6

7

8

9

Provan Residence

Melbourne, Victoria, Australia

NEOMETRO ARCHITECTS

The Provan Residence stands on a rectangular inner-suburban block, and is sited toward the southern boundary to maximize northern aspect to the living areas. The design of the house anticipated future development on the adjoining property to the north, which has since occurred. Therefore a generous first-floor terrace, that captures all-day sun, supplements the ground floor courtyard. An external stair links this stone-paved elevated terrace to the garden below. The building is a composition of interlocking, rendered planes, crowned with a copper-clad "turret."

The internal planning has two connecting living rooms on the ground floor, organized around a central stairwell. The north-facing living areas are visually ordered by six rendered blade walls placed on a 10-foot (3-meter) grid. Bedrooms are located on the first floor, with a rooftop studio opening onto a deck with views to the city skyline.

Internally, the front living room is a contemplative space with a timber floor, diffused light and views onto a small Japanese garden. The second zone, at the rear of the house, incorporates kitchen, dining and a living area focused around a fireplace. A wall of bifolding, glazed panels allows the whole interior to be opened to the courtyard. This room, flooded with daylight, is a more robust family living space with an exposed concrete floor and ceiling.

1 The Provan Residence in its suburban street setting
2 Looking from rear courtyard to elevated first-floor terrace

1

3   Second floor plan
4   First floor plan
5   Ground floor plan
6   The first-floor bedrooms open onto an elevated, stone-paved terrace
7   Front façade
8   View of main living room with an oversized pivot door providing a link to the rear part of the house beyond
9   View from dining area to the kitchen
10   The central staircase provides visual links between the levels of the house

Photography: Trevor Mein

278

1   **Living**
2   **Dining**
3   **Family**
4   **Kitchen**
5   **Pantry**
6   **Laundry**
7   **Powder room**
8   **Garage**
9   **Bedroom**
10   **Bathroom**
11   **Study**
12   **Studio**
13   **Terrace/balcony**
14   **Deck**
15   **Store**

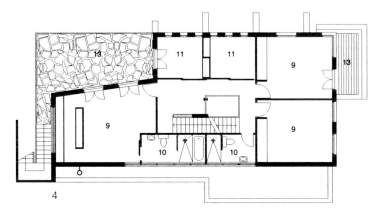

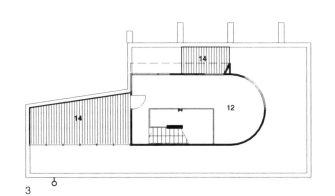

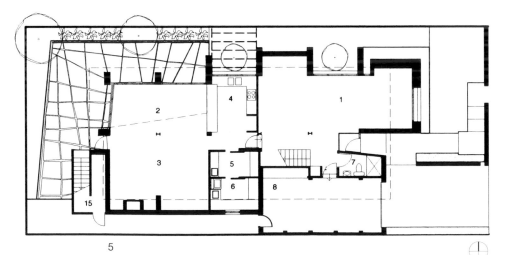

8

9

10

Quinta da Baronesa House

Bragança Paulista, São Paulo, Brazil

CLARISSA STRAUSS

Located in the countryside of São Paulo Estate, this 17,400-square-foot (1617-square-meter) contemporary house was designed as a weekend getaway for a young couple with children, and their many weekend guests.

The architect's preference is for basic, clean and natural materials. She also admires large, light, empty spaces, framed views of the landscape, and the use of water.

The recreation area was the focal point of the design, and includes two swimming pools, (one each for children and adults), a tennis court, beach volleyball facility, gym area, sauna, dressing room, barbecue and pizza oven. The clients also requested an orchard, a playground and a children's playroom that is visible from the main living room.

The house is surrounded by terraces; the kitchen is very organized, modern and streamlined. Three bedrooms were required for the family, and an additional four bedrooms were required to accommodate weekend guests.

Says the architect, "I think of architecture not as a trend or tendency; it has to live in time and be a reference of its own time. Good architecture balances form and function. That's why my architecture reflects the dreams and wishes of each client. The biggest reward for me is when the client is very happy because the project is just the way he or she wants."

1 Large glassed voids give lightness to the façade
2 Landscape and lighting at night

1

3

4

3 & 7   Large windows frame the landscape
    4   Guest bathroom
    5   Panoramic view of house from swimming pool
    6   House is surrounded by terraces
    8   A water mirror separates living room from main body of house
Photography: Luis Gomes

5

6

7

8

Remuera House

Remuera, Auckland, New Zealand

NOEL LANE ARCHITECTS

Located at the head of a north-facing valley, this house site is overlooked by adjacent housing on the south and west, with native bush to the north and on the eastern slopes. The clients' three children occupy a three-unit development located alongside the northern boundary.

These very public citizens requested extreme privacy, while wishing to take maximum advantage of existing terraces and infrastructure, outlook and site aspect.

It initially seemed logical to renovate and extend the existing house, which had been owner-occupied for many years and previously altered and extended. In fact, it was rebuilt with only the existing swimming pool, tennis court, one bedroom and study, vehicle access ways and parking areas remaining intact.

This house is sculptured around function, using solids, voids and light to hold or release space, to invite or exclude. The spaces between solids form views and light shafts that pass through the living volume, connecting and separating them from each other, and in turn unifying the three-level structure into a single readable component for the occupier. Landscape elements are used similarly with exterior retaining walls and adjacent native bush areas, visually forming the house's exterior perimeter.

Art, sculpture, collectable furniture and sports memorabilia fill these volumes with many voices. This house is finely tuned to the specific needs of two very individual people.

1 Office inside and office deck
2 North side of house looking across swimming pool
3 Entrance on north side of house

1

2

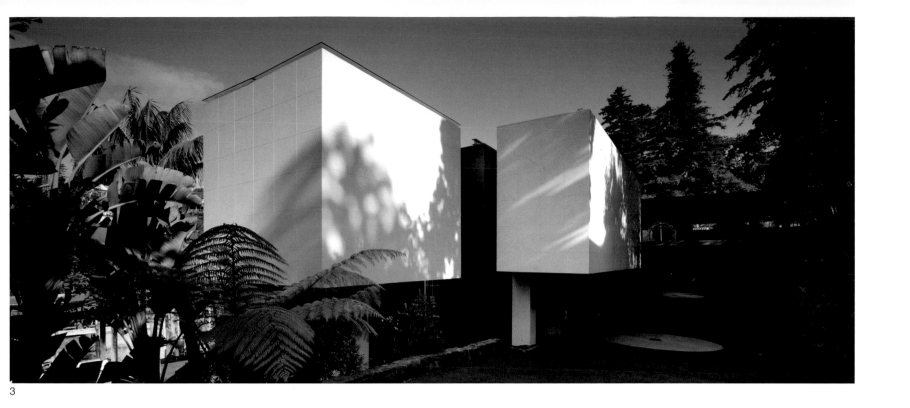

3

4

5

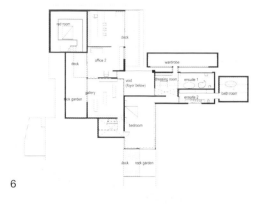

6

4   Level one floor plan
5   Level two floor plan
6   Level three floor plan
7   Gallery containing sports memorabilia
8   Squash court
9   Kitchen and living area
10 "Red room" (guest bedroom)
11 Master bedroom
Photography: Simon Devitt

7

8

9

10

11

São Paulo Residence

São Paulo, Brazil

OSCAR MIKAIL, OCTAVIO SIQUEIRA

Located in São Paulo, Brazil, this residence was designed by architect Octavio Siqueira with superb interior design by Oscar Mikail. The 12,910-square-foot (1200-square-meter) classic residence is part of an exclusive condominium in the middle of the city. Its mixed style, combining Louis XVI, Imperial, and Provincial with a contemporary flair, harmoniously blends comfort, technology, and creativity, resulting in a unique project.

The residence features sumptuous classical furniture, such as the 18th-century Venetian trumeau, the stylish 19th-century chairs, several beautiful French crystal chandeliers, and an abundance of paintings from Brazilian artists including Di Cavalcanti, Pancetti, Alfredo Volpi, Juarez Machado, and Anita Malfati.

The mix of different Italian marbles in the entrance floor is a unique feature. The stairs, designed by Mikail, are also in Calacutta marble, with a guardrail in iron and golden bronze, and are crowned by an arch in iron and bronze and a French crystal chandelier from the 19th century.

The gazebo and the swiming pool are surrounded by a beautiful garden designed by Ricardo Pinto. These are very special places for leisure, and for entertaining family and friends. The masonry gazebo has a ceiling of iron and glass, crowned by yet another crystal chandelier. The use of natural fibers, orchids, travertine marble, and pieces of ceramic tile results in a space that is both relaxed and sophisticated.

1

2

3

4

5

1 Stair guard rail in iron and golden bronze
2 Partial view of living room, with fireplace room in the background
3 Entrance hall designed by Oscar Mikail features 19th-century chandelier
4 Main façade, designed by Octavio Siqueira
5 Gazebo façade designed by Oscar Mikail; landscape by Ricardo Pinto
Photography: Alain Brugier

In a Secluded Lakeside Enclave

Mississippi, USA

KEN TATE ARCHITECT

Between a neighborhood street and a lake, this expansive stone and stucco house resonates with French imagery spanning several centuries. Much like its precedents, the residence is set behind a tall garden wall. This wall breaks to provide entry to the grounds, between two stucco pylons surmounted by an iron lantern. Containing a stone fountain, the forecourt behind the wall is a private realm in which the rambling asymmetry of the house unfolds. Its roofline and mass are divided into several volumes, including an evocative round turret standing adjacent to the entrance. Within the house, an 18th-century French chimney front, hand-hewn timbers, and classical arches recall the long history of Gallic domestic architecture from the Roman occupation onward.

At the back, the rooms open onto a loggia through arched French doors. This loggia faces the water through arched openings supported by paired Doric columns, and across a balustraded flagstone terrace. Water is brought onto the terrace by a reflecting pool bordering the lake, drawing a visual connection to the water's surface behind. As such, the experience of moving through the house is shaped by the presence of water, starting with the forecourt's fountain and extending in the reflections of the terrace's pool.

1

2

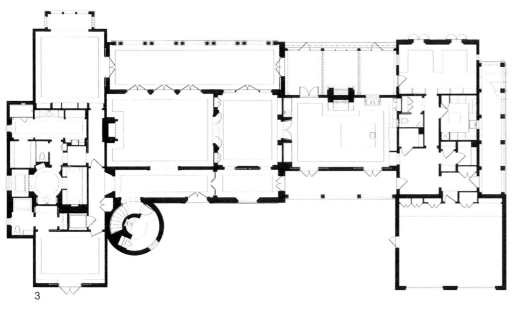

1 A walled street front typical for a house in a French village, with iron lantern and gates designed by the architect
2 Seen from across the enclave's private lake, the house, with its arcaded loggia, glows at the end of the day
3 Floor plan

3

4   A correctly scaled plaster cove mould, in the dining room,
    with limed paneling made in England from antique wood
5   Carefully preserved Bald cypress trees screen the limestone-
    columned loggia and its flagstone-paved terrace
6   The living room, as viewed from the loggia, reveals a dark
    beamed ceiling of antique oak; the brackets are English
7   A rooftop cupola illuminates the kitchen via a light well; the
    island was fashioned from antique components
Photography: Dan Bibb, Myriam Babin

4

6

7

Shelving Rock Residence

Lake George, New York, USA

BOHLIN CYWINSKI JACKSON

Set on a bluff in a dense forest overlooking Lake George, this long slender vacation and weekend house will eventually serve as a full-time residence. One essentially solid face greets visitors as they approach from the northeast along a winding lane through the trees. The other extended face is primarily glazed and affords long views of the lake and distant mountains to the southwest.

The sheltered glazed entrance on the northeast face is marked by a tall stone chimney. The plan of the 4300-square-foot (400-square-meter) house is layered in a linear fashion with the stair at its center detailed to be visually transparent. The Douglas fir framing at one side is open and the kitchen's appliance wall fits under the stair, following its stepped profile. From the entry one is drawn into the house by the extraordinary Adirondack view through the stair.

All living and sleeping spaces are organized on both levels along the glazed face of the house that overlooks the lake. The living, dining, and kitchen spaces open to each other along this face. Their relationship is heightened by a red-stained tongue of plywood panels that extends their full length. To the northeast, a recessed fireplace seating area is a counterpoint to the expansive view. To the west, the master bedroom also opens to a deck and a down slope view through the forest to a lake cove. Accessed by the open linear stair, the upper level accommodates two bedrooms and a recreation/lounge area.

The interior of the house is primarily Douglas fir; the exterior cedar siding is stained green to meld into the surrounding forest.

1   Northwest corner
2   View of house from Lake George
3   North elevation

1

2

3

4

5

6

4　View from living room
5　West elevation
6　Stair detail
7　View of living room and front entry from stair landing
Photography: Nic Lehoux

Smith Residence

Mountain Star, Avon, Colorado, USA

4240 ARCHITECTURE INC*

The client's love of European hilltop villages and adherence to strict design guidelines provided the overall concept of the house. Clustered to resemble a small mountain village, the 5000-square-foot (465-square-meter) house is an assemblage of five buildings carefully positioned on the steep forested site. The double-height, heavy timbered main building containing the great room, dining room and kitchen, was set parallel to the hillside to gain panoramic views of the distant valley and Beaver Creek ski area. The master bedroom wing was pushed forward, away from the main building and angled to provide views of the nearby meadow. This design gesture creates an outdoor living room with fireplace that the owner uses for entertaining, and screened views of the neighboring building from the great room.

Adjacent to the master bedroom wing is a 25-foot-high (7.6-meter) stone tower housing the master bathroom. At the top of the tower is a private hot tub retreat capped with a cedar trellis. A two-story building containing a two-car garage and guest suite has been set at 90 degrees to the main building, creating an entry court. Between these two wings is the fifth and smallest building, a 200-square-foot (19-square-meter) stone "wine pavilion" that houses the client's extensive 1000-bottle wine collection. This room has 12-foot-high (3.7-meter) wine racks and a rolling ladder for access. The cedar ceiling is pyramidal and capped with a copper roof and finial.

Materials were chosen to blend into the mountain setting and recall the European craftsmanship of a bygone age: buff colored stone walls, cut stone lintels and wall caps, cedar channel siding, standing-seam copper and cedar shake roofs, aluminum clad wood windows, exposed heavy-timber Douglas fir trusses and beams, knotty oak flooring, and hand-trowelled interior plaster.

*This project was completed by Urban Design Group/Inc. under the supervision of Peter Dominick, who was then a principal of Urban Design Group/Inc. Peter is now a principal of 4240 Architecture Inc. with other former principals of Urban Design Group Inc.

1   Entry court
2   View of dining terrace and outdoor fireplace
3   Study with 180-degree forest views
4   Wine pavilion with pyramid ceiling
5   Master bedroom and private terrace
6   Vaulted great room
7   Kitchen
Photography: Ken Redding

1

2

3

4

5

6

7

Solar Umbrella

Venice, California, USA

ANGELA BROOKS AND LAWRENCE SCARPA OF PUGH + SCARPA

Nestled amidst a neighborhood of single-story bungalows, the Solar Umbrella residence boldly establishes a precedent for the next generation of California modernist architecture. The addition transforms the architects' existing 650-square-foot (60-square-meter) bungalow into a 1900-square-foot (177-square-meter) residence equipped for responsible living in the 21st century.

Inspired by Paul Rudolph's 1953 Umbrella House, the Solar Umbrella provides a contemporary reinvention of the solar canopy—a strategy that provides thermal protection in climates with intense exposures. Passive and active solar design strategies render the residence 100 percent energy-neutral. Recycled, renewable, and high performance materials and products are specified throughout. Hardscape and landscape treatments are considered for their aesthetic and actual impact on the land.

The addition shifts the residence 180 degrees from its original orientation, creating a more gracious introduction to the residence and optimizing exposure to energy-rich southern sunlight. A bold display of solar panels wrapping around the south elevation and roof becomes the defining formal expression of the residence. Rather than deflecting sunlight, this state-of-the art solar skin absorbs and transforms sunlight into usable energy, providing the residence with 100 percent of its electricity.

The original bungalow is joined by a sizable addition to the south, which includes a new entry, living area, master suite, and utility room. The kitchen opens into a large living area, which opens out to a spacious front yard. An operable wall of glass at the living area delicately defines the edge between interior and exterior. A cast-in-place concrete pool provides a strong landscape element and defines the path to the front entry. At the entry, the pool cascades into a lower tier of water that penetrates and interlocks with the geometry and form of the residence. Stepping stones immersed in the water create an initiatory rite of passage into the residence as the visitor is invited to walk across water.

The master suite reiterates the strategy of interlocking space. Located directly above the new living area, up a set of floating, folded plate steel stairs, the bedroom opens onto a deep covered patio overlooking the garden. This deep porch carves out an exterior space and provides the front elevation with a distinctive character.

A dynamic composition of interlocking solids and voids creates a richly layered depth to the design. Transparency allows views to penetrate from front to back, and light penetrates at several locations. Light and shadow become palpable tools that enliven the design and help to create an effectively layered composition, rich in visual and formal interest.

1 Façade of renovated existing house
2 New entry addition showing principal living space and garden

1

3 Second floor plan
4 First floor plan
5 Dining room and kitchen beyond
6 Transition between renovated house and new addition
7 New master bedroom porch
8 Guest bathroom at ground level
9 Master bedroom and bath
Photography: Marvin Rand

5

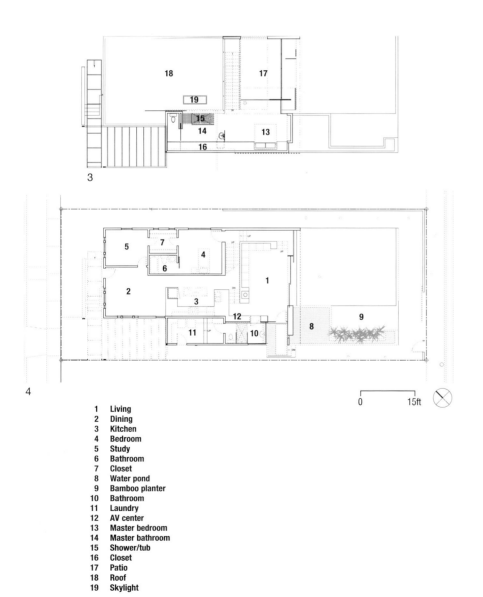

4

1 Living
2 Dining
3 Kitchen
4 Bedroom
5 Study
6 Bathroom
7 Closet
8 Water pond
9 Bamboo planter
10 Bathroom
11 Laundry
12 AV center
13 Master bedroom
14 Master bathroom
15 Shower/tub
16 Closet
17 Patio
18 Roof
19 Skylight

0   15ft

6

7

8

9

Spry House

Point Piper, New South Wales, Australia

DURBACH BLOCK ARCHITECTS

The site for the Spry House had an overwhelming view of Sydney Harbour that influenced every architectural move. So a primary question became: should the house be parallel or perpendicular to that view? The architects' preference was for the latter, with its more ambivalent relationship to the harbour; this scheme with three fluid and interweaved bands short-ending the view was the result.

It was decided to locate a large part of the brief (extra bedrooms and bathrooms, storage) within a base, on which the rest of the reduced mass of the house could be built. In this way a large clear platform, flush with the street on one side and raised on the other side, was constructed to take advantage of the views.

The intention was to make the building cloud-like, shading the living podium. Not a modernist box that hovers despite the obvious weight, but a floating mass that actually looks light enough to be there. Not at all improbable.

As the clients' accommodation requirements increased, the roof became thicker and thicker as it became more habitable. Fissures and courts were cut through the roof not only to reveal its depth, but also to receive more light, cross views and air into the living podium. The timber and glass façade here makes the wall appear impossibly delicate and ephemeral. The thinnest windows imaginable emit fleeting flickering pure green light blades throughout the space.

1

2

1   View of Sydney Harbour from pool
2   Shadow lines emphasizing the tilting panels of the back elevation
3   Close up of curved timber façade

4

5

6

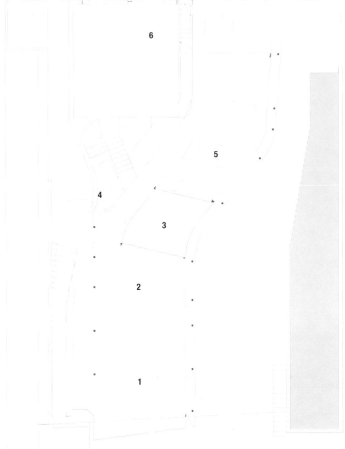

1	Living
2	Dining
3	Courtyard
4	Guest WC
5	Kitchen
6	Garage

8

4 Curved façade
5 Connection of internal living spaces
6 Skylight void above living room ceiling
7 Top of skylight
8 Ground floor plan

Photography: Brett Boardman (1,5); Anthony Browell (2–4,6,7)

Stone House

Chicago, Illinois, USA

STUART COHEN & JULIE HACKER

The house was built on a wide suburban lot that had never been built on before. The unique feature of the property was a number of large stands of mature trees. To preserve these the owners relinquished a rear lawn and the house was sited at the back of the site. This produced a driveway approach alongside a wooded yard. The house's exterior is clad entirely in a buff colored stone, with a cedar shingled roof and lime green colored casement windows and trim.

The main spaces of the house, along with a master suite, are on the main floor. The owner wanted a great room rather than separate living and dining rooms. These are visually combined into a single space with the two areas defined by changes in the direction of their beamed ceilings and by a column screen. At the end of the living room is a fireplace with translucent French doors on either side. These open into a home office and the master bedroom, which are interconnected.

The owner has four sons who were soon to go off to college. Their bedrooms plus a shared study and lounge area comprise the second floor and are tucked under the roof, giving the house a lower profile. The boys share two identical interior bathrooms, which borrow natural light through transom windows from a skylight over the central hall. The stair to the second floor continues up into a tower room, which affords views of Lake Michigan one block away.

1

1   View of house from street
2   Front entry

3

4

5

6

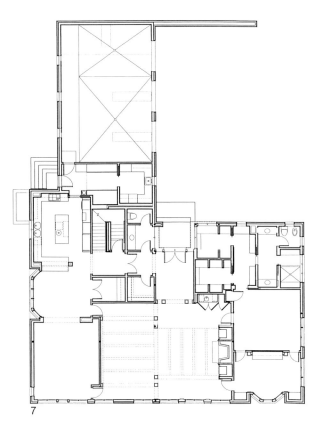

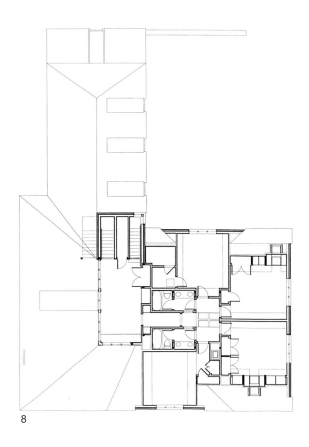

3 Entry hall
4 Kitchen
5 Second floor hall and children's bathrooms
6 Tower room
7 First floor plan
8 Second floor plan
9 Living room
10 Master closets and dressing room

Photography: Jon Miller/Hedrich-Blessing

7

8

9

10

Stone Temple in the Woods

Minnesota, USA

CHARLES R. STINSON ARCHITECTS

After a decade of living and working in Asia, the clients and their two sons were ready to return to their Minnesota roots, bringing with them the essence of their Asian experience and a vision to build not just a house, but a family retreat.

Though separated by oceans, the clients and architect were of one mind during the planning and creating process. One of the clients had grown up in a Frank Lloyd Wright home. Integrating this style and an extensive collection of Asian art, furniture and architectural pieces with the architect's compositional style was a design goal. The clients asked the architect to accompany them to Bali, to draw inspiration from the island's extraordinary architecture and detail, in turn stimulating creative ideas for the house. The clients were active and supportive during all phases of construction, obviously excited at watching their dreams realized with every new phase of the building process.

The clients worked with a friend and designer on the home's interior. The goal was to create an interior of authenticity with organic materials of glass, stone and wood. Woods ranging from exotic Brazilian walnut to reclaimed Minnesota barn wood grace the home's floors and cabinetry. The Fond du Lac stone, in and outside the home, was cut 50 percent larger than average to achieve the rugged effect present in Wright's work and Balinese temples.

According to the architect, the clients' belief in positive karma, good energy and treating people with respect, is integral to the house. "It's a retreat with a sense of homeyness, spirituality and fun."

2

1 South elevation of dark swimming pool with limestone
   surround and screened porch
2 East elevation with limestone forms and natural fir
   windows

3

4

5

3 Master suite looking south with floor-to-ceiling glass,
recessed drape pockets and indirect soffit lighting above
4 Looking west in gallery toward foyer with steps up to
dining room and steps down into living room/music
room to left
5 View looking west from stair landing toward gallery with
antique Asian columns at master suite entrance
6 Kitchen looking west with clerestory glass above
Photography: Peter Bastianelli-Kerze

6

Tan Residence

Meadow Springs, Western Australia, Australia

CHINDARSI ARCHITECTS

1 Front façade detail showing timber
window brise-soleil and vertical banding
denoting the front entry
2 The glazed rear north-facing façade
opens up to the private garden and the
golf course beyond
3 From the street, the dwelling bunkers
down protectively
4 Sunlight fills the main open-plan
living/dining/kitchen area during the
winter months
Photography: Joe Chindarsi & Robert Gordon

This tilted precast concrete house is located in a cul-de-sac, overlooking a golf course in the suburbs of Perth. Without any architectural reference point to draw from, the idea was to have the dwelling fold back in on itself, self-referencing but paradoxically contextual. The front and side walls of the house lean back at seven degrees as if buckling under the pressure/vacuum that surrounds it. From the street, the solidity of the concrete panels dissolves into glass at the rear of the building, where it opens up to take in north light and air as well as views to the garden and golfing green opposite.

The 2389-square-foot (222-square-meter) house comprises three bedrooms, a study, two bathrooms, an upper-level mezzanine, a ground level open plan living/dining/kitchen and an enclosed double garage. Given the temperate climate, the thermal mass of the concrete walls and floor slabs assist in stabilising temperatures within the dwelling. Passive solar design principles were integrated into the overall concept. As a result, there are no east- or west-facing windows. South-facing windows are small and well-protected with protruding plywood window-boxes fixed directly to the concrete panels. Extensive glazing was concentrated on the north side of the dwelling under protective overhangs—allowing solar winter gain and summer shading—as well as accessing views to the golf course.

The construction system adopted was precast concrete panels and concrete ground and suspended slabs, tied together at the top of the panels with the roof steelwork. The motivation for using this construction method was to achieve some degree of efficiency in construction time and cost, and it also afforded the architect more freedom in the design process. Almost all the precast concrete was painted externally in the shades of cream/white and internally in shades of white/gray. The external panel finish was smooth enough not to warrant the use of a textured paint, a further cost saving. The recessed banding at the main entry was simply clear-sealed to express the true color of the gray concrete panels beneath, the vestige of an original idea to leave the whole exterior of the house in its raw and natural concrete state.

1

2

3

4

Tanner Street Residence

Richmond, Victoria, Australia

ROBERT BACKHOUSE, DI RITTER, ROB GRAHAM

The Tanner Street residence sits atop a converted 19th-century warehouse, commanding uninterrupted 180-degree views of the Melbourne CBD. The new extension comprises two stories, with bedroom and bathroom facilities below and living spaces above. The two areas are dealt with quite differently, with the intimate, private realm being terraced and sheltered below the expansiveness of a completely open, floor-to-ceiling, glazed living space. To meet the demands of a heritage overlay for the area and respect the character of the existing building, the same glass type and pattern of the old warehouse windows were used.

From the moment of arrival on the lower level, all circulation paths frame a view to the outside, always maintaining a connection with the city. In contrast with the color and movement beyond the glass façade, the residence is restrained, pure and simple, with no visible details or decorative additions to compete with the rich external tapestry.

The trade-off to this emphasis on looking out is obviously the opportunity for people to look in. This has been resolved by automatic roller blinds that retract from the shadow line between the ceiling plane and the building fabric. By using a dark mesh for the blinds, privacy during the day can be achieved and views are maintained with only partial obscuring. At night, the dark mesh allows just a hint of activity, maintaining the privacy of the residents within.

The living spaces and bedrooms have been furnished rather sparingly. Furniture items have been kept to a minimum to avoid clutter, and all extraneous items are carefully concealed behind panels and within cupboards. The kitchen consists of a single built-in unit and only the presence of a sink and cooktop betray its use. Similarly the bathrooms appear to be featureless. The vanity is a made from a single piece of Corian with inset basins of the same material, and a subtle slope in the floor defines the shower base.

There are two external areas. The upper level accesses a small open deck with a discrete timber box that conceals a barbeque. This area overlooks the more expansive timber-decked terrace below, which features a stunningly positioned plunge pool. The pool edge abuts the parapet where an overflow detail distorts the horizon line between the body of water and the surrounding landscape.

The simplicity and restraint of the spaces and elements conceals a complex jigsaw of services and structure beneath, testament to the skill of the designers.

1 Plunge pool, looking west to Melbourne skyline
2 Looking west from upper-level deck into dining and lounge areas
3 Kitchen in foreground, looking over lounge and dining area

1

2

3

4

4   Lounge area with kitchen in background and fireplace hearth on right
5   View of master bedroom and ensuite from north lower deck through
     bifolding façade
6   Kitchen overlooks lounge and dining area
7   Dining area with kitchen in background
8   Lower level floor plan
9   Upper level floor plan
Photography: Earl Carter

5

6

7

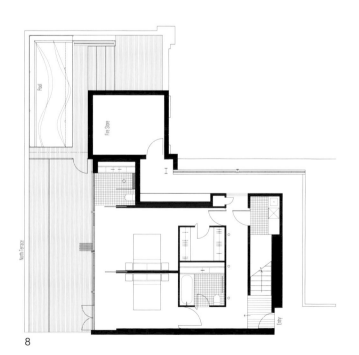

8

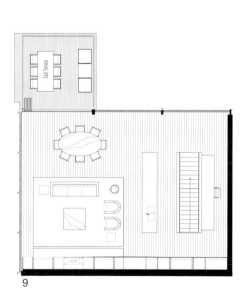

9

Tea-Tree House

Flinders, Victoria, Australia

MADDISON ARCHITECTS

The Tea-Tree House was designed as a holiday house for an extended family to occupy over short periods of time. Due to a tight budget, its size was contained to a modest 2453 square feet (228 square meters) on a half-acre (0.2-hectare) site. It was rationalised that the house could be separated into two separate volumes; a two-story square box dedicated to sleeping, and a single-story rectangular box for "living". The two boxes are connected by a slender link.

The activities zones are separated into two volumes, acting as acoustic isolators. The children are accommodated in the bunkroom with their own entertainment facilities, and the living area is used as a space for the adults. Sisal has been applied on the ceiling, contributing to the containment of noise throughout.

A predominantly lightweight timber-constructed house was considered to be the most achievable for minimising the cost and speed of construction. This lightweight construction and contained footprint recalls the fibro-cement holiday shacks found in many Australian beachside resorts in the 1960s.

The use of tea-tree battens formed the basis of the initial design. A locally sourced material, often used as fencing for coastal properties, it has been applied here in a random manner to the top and sides of the decks, acting as a privacy screen in which the dappled light evokes the notion of a relaxed seaside setting complete with barbeque. The non-linear nature of the tea-tree battens breaks down the clean lines of the refined linear boxes, while the decks extend the perceived size of the internal living spaces.

The house celebrates the modesty of a beach shack with its use of materials and the contained footprint, celebrating the ideals of a relaxed weekend residence.

1

2

3

1 Front deck – main deck leading to kitchen and living areas
2 Slender link detail
3 Front façade
4 Colored outdoor lights over deck

4

5 Rear detail – bedroom pavilion showing Ecoply-clad exterior
6 Kitchen
7 Stairs
8 Floor plans
9 Overall view of living area
Photography: Rhiannon Slatter

7

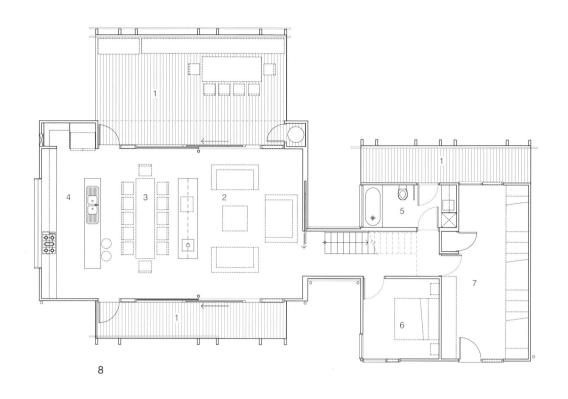

1 Deck
2 Living
3 Dining
4 Kitchen
5 Bath
6 Bed
7 Bunkroom
8 Void

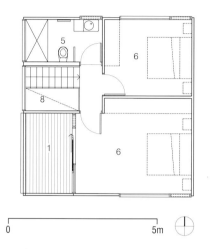

8

0   5m

Thornton House

Easton, Maryland, USA

ALFREDO DE VIDO ARCHITECTS

After a long professional relationship, the structural engineer engaged the architect to work with him on his own house. The location selected was a secluded spot on the Miles River in Talbot County on the eastern shore of Maryland. It is a popular boating, fishing, and recreational area near the Chesapeake Bay.

The architect wanted the house to reflect the owner's profession, so the resulting design has a long-span lightweight wood roof over the main space. The 40-foot (12-meter) clear span space contains the living room, dining room and kitchen. The highest point from the living room floor to the ceiling is 35 feet (11 meters).

A large, curved glass wall in the main space of the house takes full advantage of the attractive river view. It is designed to withstand the full-force hurricane winds that sweep up the coast in season. Generous overhangs protect the spaces within from summer heat and sun.

The plan divides the two separate wings connected by the high-ceilinged living space and the 7000-square-foot (650-square-meter) house can easily accommodate the owner's extended family plus a full complement of guests. In the wings, the room count includes a number of bedrooms, bathrooms, two family/media rooms, a painting studio, home offices and an attached greenhouse. Many of the rooms have direct access to outdoors.

Landscape planning concentrates on the owner's prime recreational interest, sailing. On axis with the main house is a pathway leading to a dock where the sailboat and other boats are moored. A swimming pool, tennis courts and a horse barn are also included on the grounds.

1

3

1 Entrance
2 Bowed living room and terrace
3 Entrance at night

2

1 Garage
2 Workshop
3 Greenhouse
4 Kitchen
5 Dining
6 Entrance
7 Living
8 Office
9 Exercise room
10 Master bedroom

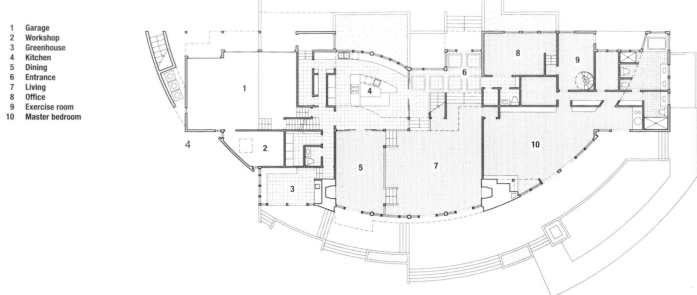

4 First floor plan
5 Pool and terrace
6 Living room
7 Second floor plan
8 Hall
9 Entrance hall
Photography: Norman McGrath (1,8); Robert Lautman (2,3,5,6,9)

5

6

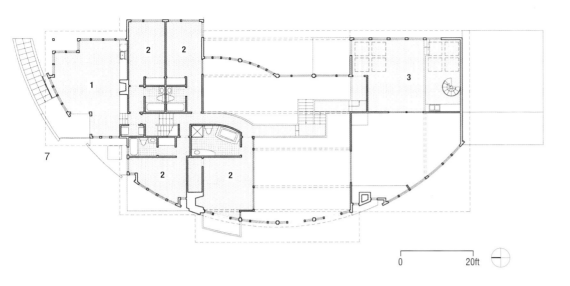

1 Studio/games room
2 Bedroom
3 Loft

7

0   20ft

8

9

Trahan Ranch

Wimberley, Texas, USA

TIGHE ARCHITECTURE

The 3200-square-foot (297-square-meter) project is situated on a 14-acre (5.7 hectare) sloped site with native oaks, natural springs, and unobstructed views. The layout of the house is a direct response to the site conditions and includes a 260-degree panoramic view. The buildings are nestled into the brow of the hill and have an unassuming appearance from afar.

A series of contradictions are explored through the architecture, including heavy and light, front and back, open and closed, and the contemporary and the vernacular. The grounded front is made of heavy materials that rise from the earth and is in sharp contrast to the more ephemeral back. The structure rises and becomes lighter at the down-slope side of the house as it opens to the landscape. The main house is a contemporary interpretation of Texas Hill Country post-and-beam construction that makes use of regional materials and the abilities of the local tradespeople. The spaces of the main house flow from one to the other with no doors while the guest room appendage has a more traditional layout.

The design includes a hydronically heated concrete slab on grade. The concrete foundation and walls provide high thermal mass. Large overhangs and covered walkways offer protection from the sun and cross ventilation is used. Natural materials are used throughout including concrete, steel, stone, and metals. Texas Hill Country limestone was picked from the site and used to create the oversized Rumford fireplace that is central to the living space. An arbor connects building components and is an armature for solar photovoltaic panels that provide power for the property. The landscape consists of regional drought-tolerant plants that are native to the area and the local ecosystem.

The steel frame structure is a kit of parts that was prefabricated in a shop and erected on site. The steel pieces attach to a series of exposed board formed reinforced concrete pylons that are a vertical extension of the foundation. A storefront aluminum glazing system of laminated opaque glass fills in the surfaces between the concrete piers and makes up the exterior walls. Exposed steel beams cantilever out from the concrete pylons and support the tilted roof plane. Steel pipe columns, splayed at unexpected angles, buttress the structure outside of the building footprint.

1

2

1 The building is nestled into the sloped site, respectful of the Texas Hill Country landscape
2 An oversized roof overhang provides sun protection for the glass-enclosed house
3 The floating roof plane rises toward the view

5

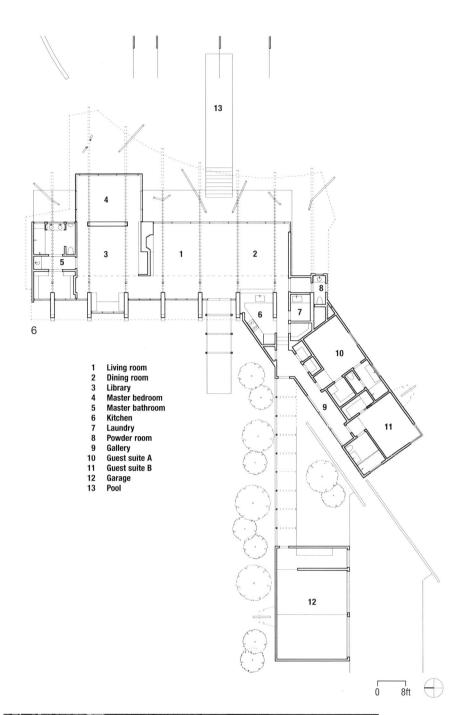

4 An oversized limestone fireplace separates the main living space from the master bedroom suite

5 A covered walkway provides shelter between building components and serves as an armature for photovoltaic panels that power the compound

6 Floor plan

7 View from dining room into kitchen with clerestory above; concrete piers grow out of the site and are visible inside

8 Structure at the back of the house becomes lighter and gently rests on the hillside

9 Sleeping quarter appendage has a powerful connection to the site with walls of glass

Photography: Art Gray

1   Living room
2   Dining room
3   Library
4   Master bedroom
5   Master bathroom
6   Kitchen
7   Laundry
8   Powder room
9   Gallery
10 Guest suite A
11 Guest suite B
12 Garage
13 Pool

0   8ft

7

8

9

Tropical Courtyard House

Singapore

GUZ ARCHITECTS

The Tropical Courtyard House is a contemporary reinterpretation of the traditional courtyard bungalow. To achieve the owner's dual requirements for privacy from the main road and views into an adjacent beautiful, tropical rain forest, the architect devised a U-shaped plan. The living/entertainment rooms and the dining/kitchen spaces form the two arms, with the staircase and bridge above acting as the link. There is a clear hierarchy to the privacy of spaces, with the children's bedrooms and master bedroom located on the upper floors. The layout of the 9684-square-foot (900-square-meter) house is disarmingly simple, and the scale of the blocks is kept low to allow for intimacy in spaces.

The architect and owner worked together to achieve spaces integrated with the landscape, allowing for the enjoyment of breeze, sun and greenery. The open design of the house, with all circulation areas opening directly into the central courtyard at the heart of the house achieves this aim. The architecture also employs a clever theatrical layering of green spaces to integrate it with the landscape beyond. The koi pond and green courtyard at the first level is a showpiece; a second-story rooftop garden is stepped behind, and the forest surrounding the site is a final backdrop. This three-tiered assemblage gives a balanced focus of nature within and without. Another special feature of the house is its attention to craftsmanship and tectonics through the materials employed and detailing of objects. One trademark is the beautiful filigree panels at the front façade. When added to the variety of intricately carved wooden doors, cabinet panels and screens, they all give a delightful play of light and shadows within and outside the house, both during the day and at night.

Nature, intimate spaces, natural materials and well-crafted details transform this residence into a tranquil retreat from the world outside.

1

2

1 View toward entrance from garage roof garden
2 Entrance
3 View back toward house from swimming pool

3

4 Main staircase looking over courtyard and koi pond
5 Bridge at upper level
6 Bamboo ceiling in veranda overlooking koi pond
7 Entrance courtyard
Photography: Luca Tettonni/guz architects

5

4

6

Vertical House

Venice, California, USA

LORCAN O'HERLIHY ARCHITECTS

Impossible to express in plan due to the constrained size of the site, this 2400-square-foot (223-square-meter) residence diverges from the pre-established response to front and back yards by balanced articulation of the skin on all faces in the vertical direction.

A simple material, cement fiber board, has been innovatively used in conjunction with three types of glazing. This allows a powerful commentary on surface manipulation, defining architecture through the envelope of a volume rather than through the volume itself. The state of hybridity in the surface formalizes the expression of a simple box while responding to the site restrictions. Verticality is again expressed in the central stair core, which extends beyond the roof for views of the Pacific Ocean, only three blocks from the site.

To increase usable square footage, the site limitations have been pushed to the maximum in both plan and height requirements, forcing the linearity of the design on paper to be translated in built form. The steel moment frame frees the skin from structural restraints, allowing an unrestricted rhythm of glazing, channel glass and solid panels. The skin illustrates the disparity of structure and envelope affected by different yet merging positions of exterior glazing. Most simply, one idea coupled with and realized through materiality defines the architecture of this residence. The impact is both powerful and artistic.

1

2

3

1 Roof sanctuary has views to Pacific Ocean
2 Detail of exterior skin and stairs
3 Exterior elevation
4 Dining room
5 Third floor plan
6 Second floor plan
7 Master bedroom
Photography: Michael Weschler

4

7

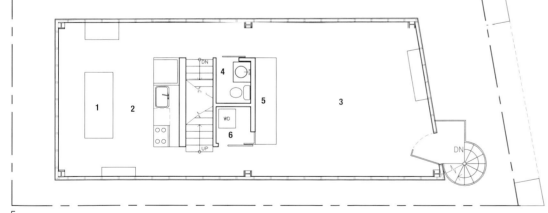

1 Dining room
2 Kitchen
3 Living room
4 Bathroom
5 Closet
6 Laundry room

5

1 Master bedroom
2 Guest bedroom
3 Bathroom
4 Closet

6

Villa Yin

Shanghai, China

HANK M. CHAO/ADAM Z.Q. SONG, MOHEN DESIGN INTERNATIONAL

This 8393-square-foot (780-square-meter) house and courtyard occupy an interior lot in Shanghai, China. The owner, one of the largest manufacturers of motorcycles in China, moved from the suburbs to this redeveloping warehouse district because of his commitment to urban living and pride in the city. The Chinese influence is seen not just in the concept but in the details of the residence.

The Chinese "looped" architectural concept is reinterpreted with medieval-like alleys that converge into a sophisticated interior layout. The traditional paired round wood columns turn into a more contemporary format set right at the entrance and draw the visitor's attention inside. The entrance alley has its own dramatic welcoming characteristics. Backlit calligraphy artworks turn into a 3D form with a metallic touch. The architects suggest that the style might be called "Chinese new modern."

1 The Chinese "looped" architecture concept layers the small separate spaces
2 Main building entrance
3 Dramatic view at the foyer
4 Courtyard is closely connected with the living room by huge revolving door panels
5 Staircase acts as a backdrop for the space
6 Indoor swimming pool
Photography: Maoder Chou

3

4

5

6

Wheatsheaf Residence

Wheatsheaf, Victoria, Australia

JESSE JUDD ARCHITECTS

The Wheatsheaf Residence investigates the nomadic nature inherent in the holiday unit. Nestled in 10 acres (4 hectares) of abandoned messmate forest, the extruded form sits at once comfortably within, and distinct from, its monoculture environment. The house examines the typology of the ephemeral, a stressed skin structure that seems to be spontaneously relocatable, perhaps informed by the Airstream trailer, an aircraft hull, or the folded steel bus shelters that dot Melbourne's southeastern suburbs.

The scheme's two parts function as both discrete and integrated elements, grounded in rudimentary internal planning. Consisting of two folded planes, the experience of the house is about the section cut. The front and rear elevations reveal the planar skins, extruded as a simple platonic gesture. The side elevations divulge little more of the womb-like interior, appearing as the simplest temporary vernacular, a corrugated iron lean-to, complete with veranda.

The primary material is simply formed corrugated steel, a floor that becomes wall and then roof. The use of black allows details to fade away—more emphasis is then placed on the main gesture. This main curved plane within the living area is lined internally in plywood, stained a red/orange that emphasizes both the warmth and the timber patterning of the ply. A train-carriage aisle/hallway connects the main space with three linear bedrooms, a severed exposition of the overall platonic volume, expressed through a primary magenta parallel entry. Ply is also used for key joinery surfaces, but here is stained a gray-brown, more akin to the surrounding forest.

The contiguous timber deck is clad in rough sawn turpentine, cut from the demolished former piers of the Wooloomooloo wharf on Sydney Harbour, and hovers uneasily over the forest floor, allowing the native wildlife to run freely under foot.

The Wheatsheaf Residence is raised above the ground; an expressed steel structure contains a deck-platform at controlled height so it does not require a balustrade. This integration is key to maintaining a desired singularity of gesture.

This is architecture as surface: three-dimensionally smooth, yet sufficiently complex to be legible through our increasingly "logo-ized" world of visual codes and conventional signs.

1 Primary magenta entry
2 Blood-red plywood interior
3 Northern aspect, deck level

1

2

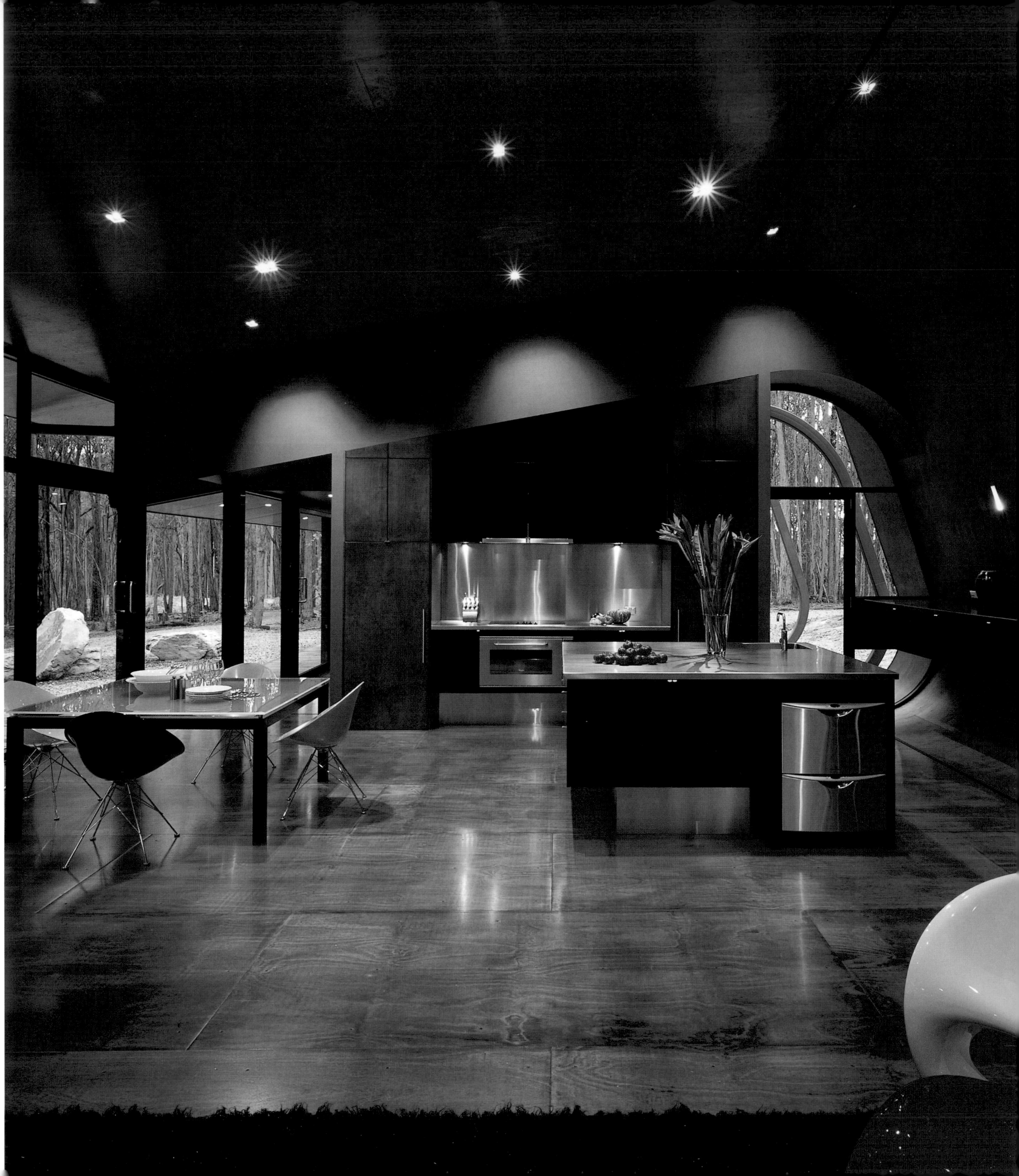

4

6

7

4   Meals area
5   Kitchen detail
6   Bathroom detail
7   Walkway to bedrooms
8   Floor plan
Photography: Peter Bennetts

5

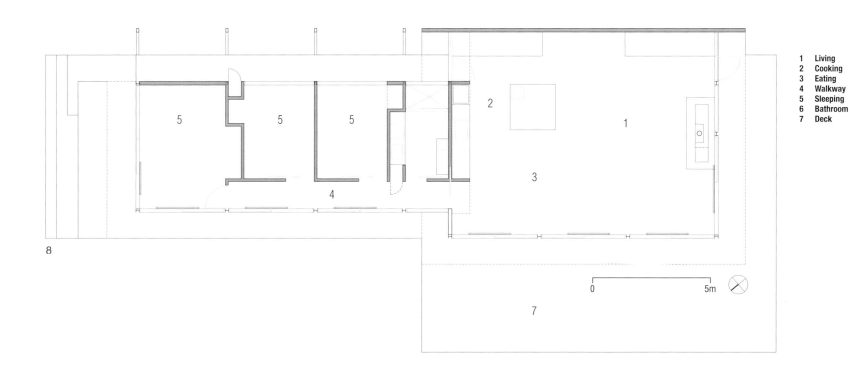

1   **Living**
2   **Cooking**
3   **Eating**
4   **Walkway**
5   **Sleeping**
6   **Bathroom**
7   **Deck**

0   5m

8

Index of Architects